the Complete 30-Day Whole Foods Instant Pot Cookbook

600 Most Essential Program-Compliant Pressure Cooking Recipes to Boost Your 30-Day Whole Foods Challenge

D1518612

Iris L. Pena

Table of Contents

People nowadays seek all types of dishes, but they all prepare in different ways. Grilling, steaming, searing, boiling, sautéing, poaching, broiling, baking, roasting, blanching, stewing, deep-frying, braising, shallow-frying, and barbecue make the entire cooking procedure more difficult for beginners who want to consume something nutritious. Today, however, everyone wants that multi-cooker known as the Instant Pot for beginners who wish to cook even at home. What exactly is an Instant Pot, and why is everyone talking about them all the time? Well, the well-known brand of multi-cookers is excellent for two reasons: it saves time and space in the kitchen. They may replace a variety of other kitchen equipment, and some can even function as a yogurt maker or sterilizer for baby bottles.

An Instant Pot is a slow cooker, rice cooker, and yogurt maker in one. Do you want to toss it in, set it, and forget it for a slow-cooker meal? That's what it'll do. Do you want to prepare your own yogurt? It'll also do that. An Instant Pot is also a multi-cooker with several functions, such as pressure cooking, slow cooking, rice cooking, steaming, warming, and sautéing — all in one gadget that speeds up the cooking process. In 2010, the first Instant Pot was released. Fast forward to today, when Instant Pots are available in a variety of sizes ranging from 3-quart to 8-quart. They're all fantastic for various reasons, but our experts agree that the Instant Pot is the best option for most people, especially because it offers low and high pressure settings. With this type of pot, the cooking time is entirely up to you.

While not every night is the same: sometimes we need a quick, easy supper to throw together at the last minute, and other days we have to rely on a slow-cooker to have dinner ready when we come home. No matter what type of day it is or how much time you have to spend on a meal, an Instant Pot adjusts. It also has a temperature self-regulating feature and sensors that can automatically detect the amount of heat and pressure, so you don't have to worry about overcooking. You can take a vacation from those quick-cooking, boneless, skinless chicken breasts if you think about soft, juicy, perfectly cooked meat in 40-90 minutes since it can cook a huge lump of meat faster than anybody else.

While the Instant Pot claims to be able to cook anything, cooking vegetables in it will be a little more difficult because high-heat steam + veggies is a recipe for limp, soggy disaster, so avoid cooking veggies like broccoli, kale, zucchini, mushrooms, and Brussels sprouts in there, and if you do, use the Quick Release to release steam.

In an Instant Pot, you can cook almost anything. Yes, proteins and vegetables are all excellent choices, but how about a massive Instant Pot pancake? What do you think of an Instant Pot cheesecake? Believe it or not, you can also perfect mac and cheese in there. Here are some more simple and delicious Instant Pot recipes: Think delicate, juicy, precisely cooked meat in 40-90 minutes, allowing you to avoid those quick-cooking, boneless, skinless chicken breasts.

If you need some more ideas to make a healthy food using only an Instant Pot, "The Complete 30-Day Whole Foods Instant Cookbook" includes lots of Instant Pot recipes to try at home. We adore these appliances enough that we dedicated an entire cookbook to it! "The Complete 30-Day Whole Foods Instant Cookbook" contains the important program-compliant pressure-cooking recipes to help you accomplish your 30-day whole foods challenge.

30-Day Whole Foods Meal Plan Challenge

Meal Plan	Breakfast	Lunch	Dinner	Motivational Quotes
Day-1	Breakfast Green Chile Bowl	Indian Chicken Tikka Masala	Lime Chicken Salad	A year from now, you will wish you started today.

Don't Put Yourself in Tempting Situations

I'm not asking you to be a hermit and tuck yourself away in a dark basement for a month, but I am telling you to be cautious of the situations you willingly put yourself in. That means don't agree to go to your favorite restaurant where you always get fried chicken and waffles and think you will eat Whole Foods . Even if you might be able to, it's a risk that's not worth taking yet.

Meal Plan	Breakfast	Lunch	Dinner	Motivational Quotes
Day-2	Sweet Potatoes with Bacon-Onion Jam	Texas Brisket Chili with Veggie	Sea Scallops and Vegetable with Aioli	With the new day comes new strength and new thoughts.

Have Strategies in Place for Your Social Life

Like I said, I'm not asking you to be a recluse. You don't have to avoid leaving the house, you just have to be smart about it! If you want a date night with your significant other, great! Do your research first and find a place you'll both be happy eating at.

Meal Plan	Breakfast	Lunch	Dinner	Motivational Quotes
Day-3	Soft-Boiled Eggs with Prosciutto Slices	Pork Char Siu with Vegetable Medley	Brazilian Fish and Shrimp Stew	Quit slacking and make shit happen.

No Fake Treats

No recreating desserts or chips or cake or whatever. I just saw a pin for a Whole30 mocha and the article suggested adding ungodly amounts of cacao and using coconut milk to make froth to recreate your chocolatey, sugary morning drink at the coffee shop. Ummmmm no.

Meal Plan	Breakfast	Lunch	Dinner	Motivational Quotes
Day-4	Sweet Potatoes with Bacon-Onion Jam	Turkey Chili with Avocado and Cilantro	Pork Shoulder and Carrot Noodle Bowls	The past cannot be changed, the future is yet in your power.

Identify Your Personal 'Food With no Brakes' and Avoid Them

What foods are triggers to old binging or mindless eating habits are different for all of us. While some people are totally fine having almond butter here or there on fruit, it's a food I couldn't keep in the house.

Day-5	Caramelized Onion and Ham Home Fries	Rich and Saucy Beef Lettuce Wraps	Tilapia Fillet with Pineapple Salsa	There's no such thing as failure: either you win, or you learn.

Leftovers, Leftovers, Leftovers

Leftovers will become your best friend. If you want an easy way to meal prep, doubling the batches of dinners you make and making that be your meal prep is a good way to go about it. It will help you reduce time spent on the whole one day meal prep strategy. Other than that, leftovers take the thinking out of what you're going to have for lunch tomorrow and make life (and decision making) a lot easier.

Day-6	Hawaiian Breakfast Hash with Bacon	Pork Ribs with Collard Greens	Salmon and Greens Salad	You will never win if you never begin.

Budget and Shop the Sales

It's no secret that healthy food is more expensive. It sucks, I know. I hate it too. But there's smart ways to shop so eating well doesn't have to break the bank. Some staple items like ghee, flours/starches, coconut aminos, and high quality oils will be necessary expenses but don't let the sticker shock scare you. Most of these things will last you a while.

Day-7	Peppery Omelet Cups	Chicken with Barbecue Sauce	Brazilian Rosemary Potato Curry	You are your only limit.

Physically Move Your Scale Out of Eyesight

So many people struggle with the rule forbidding you to weigh yourself. Even if you think you won't be tempted, you totally will be when day 20 rolls around and you're feeling ahhh-mazing. To avoid this problem all together, just do yourself a favor and put your scale up in a closet or in the trunk of your husband's car or on a high shelf in the garage.. anywhere but on the bathroom floor where you've weighed yourself everyday for years.

Day-8	Breakfast Green Chile Bowl	Coffee-Braised Beef with Guacamole	Green Beans and Potato Salad	Success is no accident: it is hard work and perseverance.

Don't Make Weight Loss the Main Goal

If you're overweight, then yes losing weight is going to help make you healthier in the long run. But you shouldn't start this program with weight loss being your primary desired outcome. Health first, weight loss second.

Day-9	Hawaiian Breakfast Hash with Bacon	Pork Sausage Loaf with Gremolata	Chicken Breast and Vegetable Soup	What you plant now, you will harvest later.

Exercise

Moving around just helps us feel better. It relieves stress and boosts our mood. Even if it's just for a short walk outside, getting your mind off all things in a way that benefits your body can be really helpful.

Day-10	Soft-Boiled Eggs with Prosciutto Slices	Lemon and Garlic Cod Fillet	Chili Pork Roast	If you know you can do better, then do better.

Change Your Mindset

Think positively going into this. This is something to celebrate! No grumbling before even starting. Celebrate and get excited about the fact that you're taking control. You picked YOU and that's super awesome. No more passively letting things happen to you anymore. You're now in the front seat.

| Day-11 | Sweet Potatoes with Bacon-Onion Jam | Lamb Steak Tagine | Vegetable Medley | It does not matter how slowly you go, as long as you don't stop. |

Time It Wisely

Eating the Whole30 way for a month is a commitment, and it may require some planning. I purposefully started mine after the holiday rush when I knew there wouldn't be too many celebrations, holidays to work around. Find a time that works for you, but don't use Thursday's happy hour as an excuse to put it off.

| Day-12 | Caramelized Onion and Ham Home Fries | Chicken Cacciatore with Zoodles | Polish Kielbasa and Cabbage Soup | Don't let a stumble in the road be the end of your journey. |

Make a Plan, and Stick with It

The key to a successful diet is to plan so that no obstacle comes as a surprise. Get sweet cravings at work? Pack your meals and plenty of snacks ahead of time so you're not going hungry. Know you'll be eating out with a friend this week? Scope out the menu for compliant options before you go.

| Day-13 | Hawaiian Breakfast Hash with Bacon | Sloppy Joe–Stuffed Mushrooms | Peppers and Egg Salad Wraps | Don't dig your grave with your own knife and fork. |

Take a Closer Look at Nutrition Labels

Sure, it's easy to avoid the junk food aisle—but what's eye-opening is the number of artificial–read: not compliant–ingredients lurking in inconspicuous foods like processed meat. Spoiler alert: There are tons of added sugar hiding in your sliced ham. Carefully inspect your food for sneaky sugars like sucrose, dextrose and maltodextrin. Unsure of an ingredient? Say hello to Google search.

| Day-14 | Peppery Omelet Cups | Chinese Five-Spice Pork Ribs | Hearty Chicken and Carrot Stew | When you eat crap, you feel crap. Keep going. |

Give Yourself a Break

For most people, completing this 30-day meal plan successfully will come down to a choice of what is most important to you: spending less money on groceries or spending less time in the kitchen. For me, given my schedule during the week, I decided I would rather spend more money on time-saving ingredient shortcuts, such as pre-cut vegetables and rotisserie chicken.

| Day-15 | Breakfast Green Chile Bowl | Chili Lime Tilapia Fillet | Beef Pot Roast | Take it one meal at a time. |

Discover New Recipes

It is the perfect time to have fun by trying new recipes. I discovered so many new favorites during the course of my 30-day Whole Foods. They all have recook value and I keep them in my personal recipe book and keep coming back to them every time I cook.

Day-16	Hawaiian Breakfast Hash with Bacon	Instant Pot Korean Beef	Mediterranean-Style Chicken Salad	When you feel like quitting, think about why you started.

Remind Yourself It's Only 30 Days

There are days you're going to want to quit. As inspiration, I would go back to these words: "Don't you dare tell us this is hard. Beating cancer is hard. Birthing a baby is hard. Losing a parent is hard. Drinking your coffee black. Is. Not. Hard." You are worth 30 days of trying something new. Armed with these tips, I know you can do it.

Day-17	Soft-Boiled Eggs with Prosciutto Slices	Pork Shoulder with Apple-Broccoli Slaw	Moringa Chicken Breast Soup	If not now, when?

Don't Binge Before You Start

"I'll start my diet on Monday" is something we all say to justify eating whatever we want. I've found that this is especially true for those who know they're going to be doing the 30-day Whole Foods and have set a date. While it's not a diet, it does still give people the feeling the world is ending and they need to cram as much food that they won't be eating into their mouth as fast as possible before they start. Don't do this. Just don't.

Day-18	Sweet Potatoes with Bacon-Onion Jam	Pulled Pork with Broccoli-Cauliflower Rice	Mexican Chicken Tinga	Fall seven times, stand up eight.

Order First at the Restaurant, No Regrets

When you go out to eat, pick a healthy option and then put the menu down. When you stare at the menu, you can easily second guess yourself, and it can trigger you to veer off course. People also change their minds when they see or hear what others have ordered. Be firm and stay committed to your plans. Be the first to order and feel great about what you ordered.

Day-19	Caramelized Onion and Ham Home Fries	Hearty Chicken and Carrot Stew	Satarash	Every step is progress, no matter how small.

Do Make a Few Freezer Meals Before You Start

I'm not saying slave away in the kitchen stock piling freezer meals for all 30 days, but I do think having a few things ready to go is beneficial. If you have some spare time, make a casserole or meatballs and put them in the freezer for the days when you get home late, didn't get to the store or simply just don't feel like cooking. For even less work, throw a soup in the crock pot and freeze it in individual portions when it's done.

Day-20	Hawaiian Breakfast Hash with Bacon	Beef and Bacon Chili	Tropically Chicken and Pineapple Salad	One pound at a time.

Raid Your Cabinets

Junk food sitting around is junk food just waiting to be eaten. If it's within sight or within reach you're just asking for unnecessary temptations and tests of willpower. Before you start, go through your cabinets, cupboards and refrigerator. Toss out, freeze, pack away or donate anything that you don't need this month.

Day-21	Peppery Omelet Cups	Pork Loin Chops with Mushroom	Chili Lime Tilapia Fillet	Never let your fear decide your future.

Sip on Herbal Teas

Non-caffeinated teas are a fun way to experience different tastes without eating garbage. Buy a tea sampler and instead of mid-meal snacks, drink some tea instead. Some of my favorite flavors are peppermint, rooibos, rosehip, lemon balm, and ginger.

Day-22	Breakfast Green Chile Bowl	Tomato-Poached Halibut Fillet	Root Vegetable and Beef Stew	It is never too late.

Eat More Soup

Counter to drinking meals from a cup, which tend to be full of sugars and mindlessly consumed, soup has been shown to be incredibly satiating. I love soup because you can make a ton of it, it's a great way to extend food, it's inexpensive, bone broth is a superfood, and you can pack a ton of vegetables into every bite.

Day-23	Caramelized Onion and Ham Home Fries	Chinese Sesame Chicken Breast	Beet and Grapefruit Salad	Leap, and the net will appear.

Keep it Simple.

Don't over meal plan or plan overly ambitious meals. Find recipes with 3-4 ingredient that you can mix-n-match throughout the week.

Day-24	Soft-Boiled Eggs with Prosciutto Slices	Pork Tenderloin Lettuce Wraps	Tuna and Tomato Chowder	The secret of change is to focus all of your energy not on fighting the old, but on building the new.

Emergency Meals.

Have emergency food on hand! Things like hard-boiled eggs, salad mix and compliant dressing or a compliant rotisserie chicken will be your best friend. In a pinch I'll even eat an avocado.

Day-25	Sweet Potatoes with Bacon-Onion Jam	Spicy Minced Lamb Meat	Salmon Fillet and Zucchini Stew	You get what you focus on, so focus on what you want.

Figure Out Your Go-To Foods:

Foods like eggs, frozen precooked shrimp, and frozen blueberries. By keeping all of these things in stock, I could whip up a quick meal if I didn't feel like cooking something huge. And the frozen blueberries were an awesome snack when I was feeling like I wanted some ice cream.

Day-26	Caramelized Onion and Ham Home Fries	Beef Cube and Sun-Dried Tomatoes	Balsamic Green Beans and Beets	Yes, I can.

Eat Enough Protein

I notice that when folks cut out their morning toast, they forget to double up on their eggs. Most people are not eating enough protein.If you aim for at least 20% of your calories from protein on a 2,000 calorie diet, that's 100 grams. This means 4-6oz of eggs, fish, red meat or poultry at each meal. Animal protein is incredibly satiating, and full of easily absorbed vitamins and minerals. (Don't confuse grams of protein with weight of meat, these are different values.)

Day-27	Hawaiian Breakfast Hash with Bacon	Hawaiian Chicken with Pineapple	Classic Shrimp Creole	Don't stop until you're proud.

Take it Easy on Fruit

you're trying to change your relationship with food and for many, this means turning off your sweet tooth. Swapping candy for multiple servings of fruit a day will not help you break your sugar addiction. Fruit is sugar. Dried fruit is even more concentrated sugar. Keep your fruit intake to one or two servings a day.

Day-28	Peppery Omelet Cups	Citrus Cinnamon Pork	Chicken Breast and Vegetable Soup	A little progress each day adds up to big results.

Avoid Drinking Your Meals

Although smoothies are technically allowed, I am not a fan of drinking calories. Science shows that your brain's normal satiety signals are bypassed when you gulp instead of chew. This means, people don't account for those calories later in the day, and end up eating more. Do yourself a favor, wake up five minutes earlier and make yourself some eggs or reheat some leftovers instead of bringing a smoothie along for your commute.

Day-29	Breakfast Green Chile Bowl	Beef and Lamb Mix with Veggie	Dill Egg and Potato Salad	It has to be hard so you'll never ever forget.

Avoid Meal Fatigue.

It's not all about sweet potatoes, bacon and avocado. Do some pre-work and save recipes so you aren't stuck eating the same thing every day.

Day-30	Sweet Potatoes with Bacon-Onion Jam	Rosemary Turkey Breast	Whole Cauliflower in Tomato-Meat Sauce	If you have discipline, drive, and determination ...nothing is impossible.

Sit Longer with Your Food

Sit down, relax, and appreciate your meal. Rushing to get the food down and watching TV while surfing Facebook is not going to help you change your relationship with food. Have a conversation with someone instead of staring at a screen. Give yourself a full 20 minutes to let your brain's satiety signals kick in before you rush up for seconds.

Introduction

Despite having hectic work schedules and lesser time for cooking at home, many people said that time is the biggest constraint that prevents them from eating right. They seldom find enough time to cook and mostly rely on takeaways and processed food. People are becoming increasingly aware of what they are consuming and what food items are best for health and well-being. They are making different efforts to prepare food with the least possible time, along with ensuring correct nutritional intake. It is, indeed, a challenge that few can succeed.

Moreover, in today's world, lifestyle-related health conditions are bothering a large section of the population. These group of people needs to be careful about how they manage their lives and accommodate food in such a way that it provides them the right dosage of nutrition without adding to calorie intake and curtailing the enjoyment of eating in terms of taste. It is another challenge, as well.

Various researches have shown that foods that are free from hydrogenated fats and artificial colors, flavors, and preservatives are useful for improving health and preventing disease. These are known as "Whole Food. "They include whole grains, fruits, vegetables, and beans, skinless chicken, nuts, and the like. Processed foods are a no-no in this group of whole food. This category of food is for those who are trying to improve their health and well-being. This also resolve the first problem of what people should eat to stay healthy.

The second problem was related to finding the time to cook at home, which seemed impossible for many due to a demanding work environment, long daily commute, the pressure of study or research, and so on. I found Instant Pot a ready solution to lower the cooking time. It is an electric powdered multi-cooker and electronically controlled, which allows them to be super easy to handle and prepare more than one item at a time.

The Ultimate 30-Day Whole Foods Instant Pot Cookbook will allow you to make some of the tastiest healthy meals on the planet and more. The book features all sorts of recipes and instructions for preparing them. We have done our very best to include a diverse set of recipes to satisfy your taste buds each day. Here you will find meals ready to be served for breakfast,lunches,dinners. These recipes include eggs, poultry, beef, lamb, pork, fish and seafood, vegetables, soups, stews, and noddle bowls for your 30 day whole food diet journey.

After you finish this book, you will find the 30-day whole foods meal plan,which will help make the road for your health goals much easier. Use this book daily as it contains a diverse set of healthy and delicious recipes that will satisfy your stomach,make you feel better and lose weight!

Chapter 1 All About Whole Food

What Is Whole Food

"Whole Foods"–that is, foods that are as close to their natural form as possible.

The term "whole food" is normally applied to vegetables, fruits, legumes and whole grains with minimal processing, but it can apply to animal foods too.

It's not as simple as neatly dividing foods into two groups – either whole foods or processed foods. Most foods we eat have undergone some degree of processing, whether it's washing, chopping, drying, freezing or canning, and that's not always a bad thing. For example, freezing and canning food gives us access to a variety of foods all year round.

Not all processing is a problem

However, there's a big difference between 'ultra-processed' and 'minimally processed' healthy foods that are close to their natural state. Whole grains, beans, fruits and vegetables are all close to the state they were in when harvested and come loaded with vitamins, minerals, fibre and other essential nutrients. But as the degree of processing and refining increases, the food's nutritional value decreases.

With more processing, the likelihood that less-beneficial ingredients like fat, salt and sugar are added goes up and the likelihood of vitamins and minerals being present goes down. The US-led National Health and Nutrition Examination Survey found that 90% of the **added sugar** in our Western diet comes from ultra-processed foods.

7 Reasons to Eat Whole Food

1. **Low in sugar**

    Some research suggests that eating sugary foods can increase your risk for obesity, insulin resistance, type 2 diabetes, fatty liver disease, and heart disease.

    Generally speaking, whole foods tend to be lower in added sugar than many processed foods.

    Even though fruit contains sugar, it's also high in water and fiber, making it much healthier option than having soda and processed foods.

2. **Heart healthy**

    Whole food is packed with antioxidants and nutrients that support heart health, including magnesium and healthy fats.

Eating a diet rich in nutritious, unprocessed foods may also help reduce inflammation, which is considered one of the major drivers of heart disease.

3. **Good for your gut**

Eating whole food may be beneficial for your gut microbiome, which refers to the microorganisms that live in your digestive tract.

Indeed, many whole foods function as prebiotics — food that your gut bacteria ferment into short-chain fatty acids. In addition to promoting gut health, these fatty acids may improve blood sugar management.

Whole food sources of prebiotics include garlic, asparagus, and cocoa.

4. **High in fiber**

Fiber provides many health benefits, including boosting digestive function, metabolic health, and feelings of fullness.

Foods like avocados, chia seeds, flaxseeds, and blackberries are particularly high in healthy fiber, alongside beans and legumes.

Consuming fiber through whole foods is better than taking a supplement as it keeps you feeling fuller longer, and you also get the added nutrients from the fruit or vegetable.

5. **Helps manage blood sugar**

Eating a diet high in fibrous plants and unprocessed animal foods may help reduce blood sugar levels in people who have or are at risk for diabetes.

6. **Good for your skin**

In addition to promoting better overall health, whole food can help nourish and protect your skin.

For instance, dark chocolate and avocados have been shown to protect skin against sun damage.

Studies suggest that eating more vegetables, fish, beans, and olive oil may help reduce wrinkling, loss of elasticity, and other age-related skin changes.

What's more, switching from a Western diet high in processed foods to one based on whole food may help prevent or reduce acne.

7. **Better for the environment**

The world population is steadily growing, and with this growth comes increased demand for food.

However, producing food for billions of people can take a toll on the environment.

This is partly due to the destruction of rainforest for agricultural land, increased fuel needs, pesticide use, greenhouse gases, and packaging that ends up in landfills.

Developing sustainable agriculture based on whole food may help improve the health of the planet by reducing energy needs and decreasing the amount of non biodegradable waste that humans produce

The Whole Food Rules

Yes: Eat real food!

Eat **meat, seafood,** and **eggs; vegetables** and **fruit; natural fats;** and **herbs, spices,** and **seasonings**. Eat foods with a simple or recognizable list of ingredients, or no ingredients at all because they're whole and unprocessed.

These foods are exceptions to the rule, and are allowed during your whole food diet.

- **Ghee or clarified butter.** These are the only source of dairy allowed during your whole food diet. Plain old butter is NOT allowed, as you may be sensitive to the milk proteins found in non-clarified butte
- **Certain legumes.** Green beans and most peas (including sugar snap peas, snow peas, green peas, yellow peas, and split peas) are allowed.
- **Coconut aminos.** All brands of coconut aminos (a brewed and naturally fermented soy sauce substitute) are acceptable, even if you see the words "coconut nectar" or "coconut syrup" in their ingredient list.
- **Fruit juice.** Some products or recipes will include fruit juice as a stand-alone ingredient or natural sweetener, which is fine for the purposes of the Whole Food diet. (We have to draw the line somewhere.)

No: Avoid for 30 days

- **Do not consume added sugar, real or artificial.** This includes (but is not limited to) maple syrup, honey, agave nectar, coconut sugar, date syrup, monk fruit extract, stevia, Splenda, Equal, Nutrasweet, and xylitol. If there is added sugar in the ingredient list, it's out.
- **Do not eat grains.** This includes (but is not limited to) wheat, rye, barley, oats, corn, rice, millet, bulgur, sorghum, sprouted grains, and all gluten-free pseudo-cereals like quinoa, amaranth, and buckwheat. This also includes all the ways we add wheat, corn, and rice into our foods in the form of bran, germ, starch, and so on. Again, read your labels.
- **Do not eat most forms of legumes.** This includes beans (black, red, pinto, navy, garbanzo/chickpeas, white, kidney, lima, fava, cannellini, lentils, adzuki, mung, cranberry, and black-eyes peas); peanuts (including peanut butter or peanut oil); and all forms of soy (soy sauce, miso, tofu, tempeh, edamame, soy protein, soy milk, or soy lecithin).
- **Do not eat dairy.** This includes cow, goat, or sheep's milk products like milk, cream, cheese, kefir, yogurt, sour cream, ice cream, or frozen yogurt.
- **Do not consume baked goods,** junk foods, or treats with "approved" ingredients. These are the same foods that got you into health-and-craving trouble in the first place—and a pancake is still a pancake, even if it's made with coconut flour.
- **Do not consume alcohol,** in any form, not even for cooking. (And ideally, no tobacco products of any sort, either.)

Chapter 2 Use Instant Pot in Whole Food Cooking

What is Instant Pot?

Instant Pot is an electric pressure cooker with seven cooking functions, which differs from many kitchen appliances with only one purpose. The Instant Pot does pressure cooking, rice cooking, browning, slow cooking, sautéing. It keeps the food warm. There is a handy yogurt button for making yogurt. It contains a 6-liter stainless steel pot that is big enough to prepare soups and stews several times. Besides, it is easy to clean.

The Benefit of using Instant Pot

Saving Time & Energy:

The Instant Pot speeds up cooking by two to six times, making it extremely energy-efficient, while preserving nutrients and resulting in healthy, tasty dishes. The Instant Pot is the fastest, easiest, most foolproof way to get these done. Two key factors contribute to the energy efficiency of instant pot:

lThe cooking compartment (the inner Pot) is wholly insulated so that it needs less energy to warm up.

lInstant pot use much less liquid than traditional cooking methods, so they boil faster.

Keep Vitamins and Nutrients Intact:

Cooking (like ordinary steam) can result in the elimination of water-soluble vitamins from foods, thereby reducing their nutritional value. Instant Pot cook food quickly, thoroughly, and evenly, allowing food to store up to 90% of these water-soluble vitamins .

It makes food more flavorful:

When you cook meat with a large quantity of spices, pressure cooking helps infuse the meat with additional flavor. One of the things you realize with whole food especially when you're eating what seems to be your hundredth piece of chicken for the week—is that spices are what keep it interesting. The pressure cooker allows spice flavors to meld together quickly, and the resulting taste is like that of slow-cooked meat.

Eliminate Harmful Microorganisms:

By creating an environment where water can boil at temperatures above 212°F, Instant Pot cookers are characterized by their versatile ability to kill off harmful bacteria effectively.

Safety:

Traditional pressure cookers can be dangerous, sometimes they can explode if the heat is not turned off at the right time. With the instant pot there is no danger! Thanks to Keep Warm mode after cooking function.

Digestibility:

Pressure cook is excellent for those suffering from gastrointestinal disorders after consuming beans. The compounds in the beans that cause the disturbance are reduced due to pressure cooking with consequent more comfortable digestion.

It is Convenient:

Cooking is very simple. You can easily put your ingredients in the pot, close the lid, set the cooking mode and time, and have a delicious dish in minutes. Thanks to the pressure flow inside the pot, the meals are cooked evenly, with no cooked parts or burnt edges. In addition, it is easy to clean and maintain. You can remove stubborn grease with a little white vinegar and a mild soap solution.

It simplifies cleanup:

In keeping with my "I am lazy/I am efficient" mode, I love having only one pot to clean when I'm done cooking.

Chapter 3 Breakfast

Hawaiian Breakfast Hash with Bacon

Prep time: 10 minutes | Cook time: 3 minutes | Serves 6

4 whole30 approved bacon strips, chopped
1 tablespoon canola or coconut oil
2 large sweet potatoes, peeled and cut into
    ½-in. pieces
1 cup water
2 cups cubed fresh pineapple (½-in. cubes)
½ teaspoon salt
¼ teaspoon chili powder
¼ teaspoon paprika
¼ teaspoon pepper
⅛ teaspoon ground cinnamon

1. Select the saute or browning setting on a 6-qt. electric pressure cooker; adjust for medium heat. Add bacon; cook and stir until crisp. Remove with a slotted spoon; drain on paper towels. Discard drippings.
2. Add oil to pressure cooker. When oil is hot, brown sweet potato pieces in batches. Remove from pressure cooker. Add water to pressure cooker. Cook 1 minute, stirring to loosen browned bits from pan. Press cancel. Place steamer basket in pressure cooker.
3. Stir pineapple and seasonings into potatoes; transfer to steamer basket. Lock lid; close pressure-release valve. Adjust to pressure cook on high for 2 minutes. Quick-release pressure. Sprinkle with the bacon.

Sweet Potatoes with Bacon-Onion Jam

Prep time: 10 minutes | Cook time: 20 minutes | Serves 4 to 6

1 tablespoon extra-virgin olive oil
7 slices thick-cut whole30 approved
    bacon, diced
1 yellow onion, diced
1 teaspoon Worcestershire sauce
¼ cup beef stock
3 (19-ounce /538.6-g total) sweet
    potatoes, peeled and cut into
    large cubes
⅓ cup water
Salt and freshly ground black
    pepper, to taste
¼ teaspoon cayenne pepper

1. Press sauté on the Instant Pot. Make sure the display light is beneath normal. Once the pot reads "hot," add the olive oil and bacon. Sauté for about 10 minutes, or until crispy, stirring regularly to prevent sticking.
2. Add the onion and sauté for an additional 5 to 7 minutes, or until the onion is starting to caramelize.
3. Deglaze the pot with the Worcestershire and beef stock. Use the edge of a wooden spoon to scrape up all the browned bacon bits from the bottom of the pot. Sauté for 2 more minutes.
4. Press cancel. Stir in the sweet potatoes along with the water, plus salt and black pepper to taste.
5. Secure the lid with the steam vent in the sealed position. Press pressure cook until the display light is beneath high pressure. Use the plus and minus buttons to adjust the time until the display reads "3 minutes." When the timer sounds, quick release the pressure.
6. Stir in the cayenne pepper. Let the potato mixture cool slightly before tasting and adjusting the salt and pepper, if needed.

Soft-Boiled Eggs with Prosciutto Slices

Prep time: 5 minutes | Cook time: 3 minutes | Serves 2

1 cup water
4 large eggs
1 teaspoon truffle salt
8 slices prosciutto

1. Pour the water into the Instant Pot and insert the steam trivet. Carefully place the eggs on the trivet.
2. Secure the lid with the steam vent in the sealed position. Press manual and immediately adjust the timer to 3 minutes. Check that the display light is beneath high pressure.
3. When the timer sounds, quick release the pressure and carefully remove the lid. Run the eggs under cold water until cool, then peel.
4. Sprinkle the eggs with truffle salt. Serve with the prosciutto slices.

Breakfast Green Chile Bowl

Prep time: 10 minutes | Cook time: 1½ hours | Serves 8

3 pounds (1.4 kg) pork shoulder
1½ teaspoon cumin
Salt and pepper, to taste
3 tablespoons bacon fat
1 onion, chopped
¾ cup chicken broth
1 can crushed tomatoes
2 milk hatch green chilies
2 hot hatch green chilies
1 avocado, sliced

1. Season the pork with cumin, salt, and pepper. Set aside.
2. Press the Sauté button on the Instant Pot and melt the bacon fat.
3. Sauté the onions and add the seasoned pork. Stir for 3 minutes then add the chicken broth, tomatoes, and chilies.
4. Close the lid and seal off the vent.
5. Press the Manual button and adjust the cooking time to 90 minutes.
6. Do quick pressure release and shred the pork using two forks.
7. Place the shredded pork into breakfast bowls and garnish with avocado slices on top.

Caramelized Onion and Ham Home Fries

Prep time: 10 minutes | Cook time: 15 minutes | Serves 4 to 6

1 tablespoon extra-virgin olive oil
2 tablespoons ghee or clarified butter
2 yellow onions, diced
¾ cup diced thick-cut ham
½ teaspoon chopped fresh rosemary
3 sprigs thyme
3 large russet potatoes, cut into 1" cubes
Salt and freshly ground black pepper, to taste
¼ cup chicken stock

1. Press sauté and make sure the display light is beneath normal. Wait a minute or two for the pot to heat. Add the olive oil and butter. Once the butter melts, add the onions. Cook for about 9 minutes, or until the onions start to caramelize.
2. Add the ham, rosemary and thyme. Stir to combine. Sauté for another 3 minutes.
3. Press cancel. Stir in the potatoes, salt and pepper to taste and the stock. Using a wooden spoon, scrape up any bits from the bottom of the pan.
4. Secure the lid with the steam vent in the sealed position. Press pressure cook until the display light is beneath high pressure. Use the plus and minus buttons to adjust the time until the display reads "3 minutes." When the timer sounds, quick release the pressure.
5. Remove the lid, stir and add more salt or pepper if needed.

Peppery Omelet Cups

Prep time: 5 minutes | Cook time: 5 minutes | Serves 2

½ teaspoon olive oil
3 eggs, beaten
1 cup water
Salt and freshly ground black pepper, to taste
1 onion, chopped
1 jalapeño pepper, chopped

1. Prepare two ramekins by adding a drop of olive oil in each and rubbing the bottom and sides.
2. In a medium bowl, whisk together the eggs, water, salt and black pepper until combined.
3. Add the onion and jalapeño, stir.
4. Transfer egg mixture to the ramekins.
5. Prepare the Instant Pot by adding the water to the pot and placing the steam rack in it.
6. Place the ramekins on the steam rack and secure the lid.
7. Close and lock the lid. Select MANUAL and cook at HIGH pressure for 5 minutes.
8. When the timer goes off, use a Quick Release. Carefully unlock the lid.
9. Serve hot.

Beef Taco

Prep time: 10 minutes | Cook time: 16 minutes | Serves 6

1 teaspoon coconut oil
2 cups ground beef
1 teaspoon chili flakes
3 jalapeño peppers, chopped
2 eggs, beaten
½ avocado, chopped
¾ cup black olives, sliced
⅓ cup coconut milk

1. Press the Sauté button on the Instant Pot and melt the coconut oil for 2 minutes.
2. Add the ground beef and chili flakes to the pot and sauté for 4 minutes, or until lightly browned, stirring constantly. Stir in the remaining ingredients. Set the lid in place.
3. Select the Manual mode and set the cooking time for 10 minutes on High Pressure.
4. When the timer goes off, do a quick pressure release. Carefully open the lid. Serve immediately.

Coconut and Pumpkin Seed Porridge

Prep time: 10 minutes | Cook time: 5 minutes | Serves 4

½ cup chopped almonds
4 tablespoons shredded unsweetened coconut
2 tablespoons flaxseed
2 tablespoons pumpkin seeds
1 teaspoon ground cinnamon
½ teaspoon grated nutmeg
¼ teaspoon ground cloves
Himalayan salt, to taste
1 cup boiling water

1. Add all the ingredients to the Instant Pot and stir to combine. Set the lid in place.
2. Select the Manual mode and set the cooking time for 5 minutes on High Pressure.
3. When the timer goes off, do a quick pressure release. Carefully open the lid. Serve immediately.

Creamy Beef and Cabbage Bowl

Prep time: 10 minutes | Cook time: 7 minutes | Serves 4

1 tablespoon avocado oil
1 pound (454 g) ground beef
1 clove garlic, minced
½ teaspoon sea salt
½ teaspoon ground black pepper
½ teaspoon ground turmeric
¼ teaspoon ground cinnamon
¼ teaspoon ground coriander
¼ cup almond butter
½ cup full-fat coconut milk
1 small head green cabbage, shredded

1. Press the Sauté button on the Instant Pot and heat the oil. Crumble in the ground beef and cook for 3 minutes, breaking up the meat with a wooden spoon or meat chopper.
2. Stir in the garlic, salt, black pepper, turmeric, cinnamon, and coriander. Add the almond butter and coconut milk. Stir constantly until the almond butter melts and mixes with the coconut milk.
3. Layer the cabbage on top of the meat mixture but do not stir. Set the lid in place. Select the Manual mode and set the cooking time for 4 minutes on High Pressure.
4. When the timer goes off, do a quick pressure release. Carefully open the lid. Stir the meat mixture.
5. Taste and adjust the salt and black pepper, and add more red pepper flakes if desired. Use a slotted spoon to transfer the mixture to a serving bowl. Serve hot.

Walnut and Pecan Granola

Prep time: 10 minutes | Cook time: 2 minutes | Serves 12

2 cups chopped raw pecans
1¾ cups vanilla-flavored egg white protein powder
1¼ cups unsalted butter, softened
1 cup sunflower seeds
½ cup chopped raw walnuts
½ cup slivered almonds
½ cup sesame seeds
½ cup Swerve
1 teaspoon ground cinnamon
½ teaspoon sea salt

1. Add all the ingredients to the Instant Pot and stir to combine. Lock the lid, select the Manual mode and set the cooking time for 2 minutes on High Pressure.
2. When the timer goes off, do a natural pressure release for 10 minutes, then release any remaining pressure.
3. Open the lid. Stir well and pour the granola onto a sheet of parchment paper to cool.
4. It will become crispy when completely cool. Serve the granola in bowls.

Cabbage and Beef Breakfast Bowl

Prep time: 10 minutes | Cook time: 7 minutes | Serves 4

1 tablespoon avocado oil
1 pound (454 g) ground beef
1 clove garlic, minced
½ teaspoon sea salt
½ teaspoon ground black pepper
½ teaspoon ground turmeric
¼ teaspoon ground cinnamon
¼ teaspoon ground coriander
¼ cup almond butter
½ cup full-fat coconut milk
1 small head green cabbage, shredded

1. Press the Sauté button on the Instant Pot and heat the oil. Crumble in the ground beef and cook for 3 minutes, breaking up the meat with a wooden spoon or meat chopper.
2. Stir in the garlic, salt, black pepper, turmeric, cinnamon, and coriander. Add the almond butter and coconut milk. Stir constantly until the almond butter melts and mixes with the coconut milk.
3. Layer the cabbage on top of the meat mixture but do not stir. Set the lid in place. Select the Pressure Cook mode and set the cooking time for 4 minutes on High Pressure.
4. When the timer goes off, do a quick pressure release. Carefully open the lid. Stir the meat mixture.
5. Taste and adjust the salt and black pepper, and add more red pepper flakes if desired. Use a slotted spoon to transfer the mixture to a serving bowl. Serve hot.

Apple Smoothie

Prep time: 5 minutes | Cook time: 3 minutes | Makes 5 cups

7 medium apples (about 3 pounds / 1.4 kg), peeled and cored
½ cup water
½ cup sugar
1 tablespoon lemon juice
¼ teaspoon vanilla extract

1. Slice each apple into 8 wedges on your cutting board, then slice each wedge crosswise in half.
2. Add the apples to the Instant Pot along with the remaining ingredients. Stir well. Secure the lid. Select the Pressure Cook mode and set the cooking time for 3 minutes at High Pressure.
3. Once cooking is complete, do a natural pressure release for 10 minutes, then release any remaining pressure.
4. Carefully open the lid. Blend the mixture with an immersion blender until your desired consistency is achieved. Serve warm.

Hawaiian Sweet Potato Hash

Prep time: 10 minutes | Cook time: 20 minutes | Serves 6

4 bacon strips, chopped
1 tablespoon canola or coconut oil
2 large sweet potatoes, peeled and cut into ½-inch pieces
1 cup water
2 cups cubed fresh pineapple
½ teaspoon salt
¼ teaspoon paprika
¼ teaspoon chili powder
¼ teaspoon pepper
⅛ teaspoon ground cinnamon

1. Press the Sauté button on the Instant Pot and add the bacon. Cook for about 7 minutes, stirring occasionally, or until crisp.
2. Remove the bacon with a slotted spoon and drain on paper towels. Set aside. In the Instant Pot, heat the oil until it shimmers.
3. Working in batches, add the sweet potatoes to the pot and brown each side for 3 to 4 minutes.
4. Transfer the sweet potatoes to a large bowl and set aside. Pour the water into the pot and cook for 1 minute, stirring to loosen browned bits from pan.
5. Place a steamer basket in the Instant Pot. Add the pineapple, salt, paprika, chili powder, pepper, and cinnamon to the large bowl of sweet potatoes and toss well, then transfer the mixture to the steamer basket. Secure the lid.
6. Select the Steam mode and set the cooking time for 2 minutes at High Pressure. Once cooking is complete, do a quick pressure release. Carefully open the lid. Top with the bacon and serve on a plate.

Lemony Applesauce

Prep time: 5 minutes | Cook time: 3 minutes | Makes 5 cups

7 medium apples (about 3 pounds / 1.4 kg), peeled and cored
½ cup water
½ cup sugar
1 tablespoon lemon juice
¼ teaspoon vanilla extract

1. Slice each apple into 8 wedges on your cutting board, then slice each wedge crosswise in half. Add the apples to the Instant Pot along with the remaining ingredients.
2. Stir well. Secure the lid. Select the Manual mode and set the cooking time for 3 minutes at High Pressure.
3. Once cooking is complete, do a natural pressure release for 10 minutes, then release any remaining pressure.
4. Carefully open the lid. Blend the mixture with an immersion blender until your desired consistency is achieved. Serve warm.

Corn and Sweet Potato Scramble

Prep time: 10 minutes | Cook time: 8 hours | Serves 2

1 teaspoon butter, at room temperature, or extra-virgin olive oil
4 eggs
½ cup 2% milk
⅛ teaspoon sea salt
½ teaspoon smoked paprika
½ teaspoon ground cumin
Freshly ground black pepper, to taste
1 cup finely diced sweet potato
1 cup frozen corn kernels, thawed
½ cup diced roasted red peppers
2 tablespoons minced onion

1. Grease the inside of the Instant Pot with the butter. In a small bowl, whisk together the eggs, milk, salt, paprika, and cumin.
2. Season with the freshly ground black pepper. Put the sweet potato, corn, red peppers, and onion into the Instant Pot.
3. Pour in the egg mixture and stir gently. Cover and press the Slow Cook button, and cook on low for 8 hours or overnight. (Press Slow Cook again to toggle between Low and High cooking temperatures.) Serve warm.

Green Veggie Frittata

Prep time: 5 minutes | Cook time: 15 minutes | Serves 4

1 tablespoon coconut oil or ghee
8 eggs
⅓ cup coconut cream or full-fat coconut milk
½ teaspoon sea salt
½ teaspoon freshly ground black pepper
½ teaspoon chili powder
¼ cup green bell pepper, diced
3 scallions, both white and green parts, chopped
½ cup packed fresh baby spinach
1 large avocado, sliced

1. Grease the bottom and sides of a 6- or 7-inch heatproof dish that fits in the bowl of your Instant Pot with the oil. Set aside.
2. In a medium bowl or food processor, whisk together the eggs, coconut cream, salt, black pepper, and chili powder until fluffy. Add the bell pepper, scallions, and spinach. Stir to combine. Pour the mixture into the prepared dish and cover with foil.
3. Pour 1½ cups of water into the bowl of the Instant Pot. Place a trivet in the bottom of the pot. Place the dish containing the frittata on the trivet.
4. Secure the lid and seal the vent. Select Pressure Cook or Manual and cook on high pressure for 12 minutes, then allow the pressure to naturally release for 15 minutes. Quick release the remaining pressure in the pot and remove the lid. If not done to your liking, cook for an additional 5 minutes at high pressure, followed by a quick release.
5. When cool enough to handle, top with avocado slices to serve.

Spicy Sausage and "No-tato" Hash

Prep time: 8 minutes | Cook time: 25 minutes | Serves 3

1 tablespoon extra-virgin olive oil
16 ounces uncooked chorizo
2 garlic cloves, minced
1 yellow onion, diced
½ teaspoon dried rosemary
1 cup chicken broth
3 medium sweet potatoes, peeled and cut into bite-size pieces
½ teaspoon freshly ground black pepper
1 tablespoon balsamic vinegar

1. Select Sauté on the Instant Pot. Heat the oil until it shimmers.
2. Sauté the chorizo, garlic, onion, and rosemary for 3 to 5 minutes until browned, stirring occasionally. Press Cancel.
3. Pour the broth into the pot. Use a wooden spoon to scrape up any pieces of food stuck to the bottom. Add the sweet potatoes to the pot and stir to combine.
4. Secure the lid and seal the vent. Select Pressure Cook or Manual and cook on high pressure for 10 minutes, then allow the pressure to naturally release for 10 minutes. Quick release any remaining pressure in the pot and remove the lid.
5. Stir in the pepper and vinegar and enjoy.

Coconut-Blueberry Chia Porridge

Prep time: 5 minutes | Cook time: 10 minutes | Serves 3

1 (14-ounce) can full-fat coconut milk
½ cup chia seeds
½ cup any type of nut, or a mix
¼ cup pumpkin seeds
¼ cup pure maple syrup or raw honey
½ teaspoon ground cinnamon
½ teaspoon pure vanilla extract
2 cups fresh blueberries

1. Pour 1½ cups of water into the bowl of the Instant Pot. Place a trivet in the pot.
2. In a heatproof bowl or dish that fits inside the bowl of your Instant Pot, combine the coconut milk, chia seeds, nuts, pumpkin seeds, maple syrup, cinnamon, vanilla, and ½ cup of water. Stir in the blueberries and place the bowl on the trivet.
3. Secure the lid and seal the vent. Select Pressure Cook or Manual and cook on high pressure for 5 minutes, then allow the pressure to naturally release for 5 minutes. Quick release any remaining pressure in the pot and remove the lid. The porridge will thicken as it cools.

Sweet Potato Breakfast Bowls

Prep time: 5 minutes | Cook time: 15 minutes | Serves 3

1 sweet potato, peeled and chopped
1 apple or pear, cored and chopped
½ cup nondairy milk
2 tablespoons nut or seed butter
(almond, cashew, sunflower)
¼ teaspoon ground cinnamon
Pinch ground nutmeg

1. In a 6-or 7-inch heatproof dish that fits inside the bowl of your Instant Pot, combine the sweet potatoes and apples.
2. Put a trivet in the pot and pour in 1½ cups of water. Set the dish on the trivet. Secure the lid and seal the vent. Select Pressure Cook or Manual and cook on high pressure for 6 minutes, then allow the pressure to naturally release for 10 minutes. Quick release any remaining pressure in the pot and remove the lid.
3. Add the milk, nut butter, cinnamon, and nutmeg to the bowl. Use an immersion or regular blender to combine, or leave chunky. Add more milk if needed. Serve hot in bowls.

Sweet Oatmeal with Yummy Blueberries

Prep time: 5 minutes | Cook time: 3 minutes | Serves 2

1 cup old-fashioned rolled oats
2 cups water
1 cup blueberries
2 tablespoon sunflower seeds
2 tablespoon agave nectar

1. Add all the Ingredients except blueberries to Instant Pot.
2. Secure the lid of instant pot and press *Manual* function key.
3. Adjust the time to 3 minutes and cook at high pressure,
4. When it beeps; release the pressure naturally and remove the lid.
5. Stir the prepared oatmeal and serve in a bowl. Garnish with blueberries on top.

Browned Spiced Carrots with Garam Masala

Prep time: 10 minutes | Cook time: 25 minutes | Serves 4

2 and ½ pounds (1.133 kg) carrots,
sliced
3 tablespoons avocado oil
Salt and black pepper, to taste
1 cup veggie stock
1 teaspoon garam masala
½ teaspoon sweet chili powder
1 teaspoon rosemary, dried

1. Set your instant pot on Sauté mode, add the oil, heat it up, add the carrots and brown for 5 minutes.
2. Add the rest of the ingredients, put the lid on and cook on High for 10 minutes.
3. Release the pressure naturally for 10 minutes, divide the mix between plates and serve as a side dish.

Chapter 4 Eggs

Poached Egg Cups

Prep time: 5 minutes | Cook time: 5 minutes | Serves 5

5 eggs
1 cup water

1. Place a trivet or steamer basket inside the Instant Pot and pour water over.
2. Spray 5 silicone cups with cooking spray.
3. Crack each egg into each greased cup.
4. Place the silicone cups with eggs on the steamer.
5. Close the lid.
6. Press the Steam button and adjust the cooking time to 5 minutes.
7. Do quick pressure release.

Delightful Soft Eggs with Ham

Prep time: 10 minutes | Cook time: 4 minutes | Serves 4

3 eggs
1 teaspoon salt
½ teaspoon ground white pepper
1 teaspoon paprika
1 cup water
6 ounces (170 g) ham
2 tablespoons chives
¼ teaspoon ground ginger

1. Beat the eggs into the small ramekins.
2. Season with the salt, pepper, and paprika.
3. Prepare the Instant Pot by adding the water to the pot and placing the steam rack on top.
4. Place the ramekins on the steam rack and secure the lid.
5. Select the STEAM setting and set the cooking time for 4 minutes.
6. Meanwhile, chop the ham and chives and combine the ingredients together. Add ground ginger and stir the mixture.
7. Transfer the mixture to the serving plates.
8. When the timer beeps, use a Quick Release. Carefully unlock the lid.
9. Serve the eggs over the ham mixture.

Hard-Boiling Eggs

Prep time: 5 minutes | Cook time: 5 minutes | Serves 6

6 eggs
Ice

1. Pour 1 cup water into the Instant Pot and arrange the handled trivet on the bottom. Place the eggs in a single layer on top of the trivet. Secure the lid and move the steam release valve to Sealing. Select Manual/Pressure Cook to cook on high pressure for 4 minutes for runny yolks or 5 minutes for completely hard-cooked yolks.
2. While the eggs are cooking, fill a large bowl with ice and water to create an ice water bath for the eggs.
3. Once the cooking cycle has ended, for runny yolks, immediately move the steam release valve to Venting to quickly release the pressure. When the floating valve drops, remove the lid and use tongs to transfer the eggs to the ice water bath to stop the cooking process. (This prevents the green ring around the yolk.) For completely hard-cooked yolks, don't open the lid right away. Let the pressure naturally release for 5 minutes, then move the steam release valve to Venting and release the remaining pressure. Transfer the eggs to the ice water bath.
4. Let the eggs cool in the ice water bath for 5 minutes, then peel and serve, or store them in an airtight container in the fridge for 1 week. I find that the eggs are easiest to peel immediately after removing them from the ice water bath, so you may want to peel them all right away, even if you plan on storing some of them in the fridge for later.

Dill-Pepper Deviled Eggs

Prep time: 10 minutes | Cook time: 4 minutes | Makes 2 dozen

1 cup cold water
12 large eggs
⅔ cup Whole30-compliant mayonnaise
4 teaspoons dill pickle relish
2 teaspoons snipped fresh dill
2 teaspoons Whole30-compliant Dijon mustard
1 teaspoon coarsely ground pepper
¼ teaspoon garlic powder
⅛ teaspoon paprika or cayenne pepper

1. Pour water into 6-qt. electric pressure cooker. Place trivet in cooker; set eggs on trivet. Lock lid; make sure vent is closed. Select manual setting; adjust pressure to low, and set time to 4 minutes. When finished cooking, allow pressure to naturally release for 5 minutes; quick-release any remaining pressure according to manufacturer's directions. Immediately place eggs in a bowl of ice water to cool.
2. Cut eggs lengthwise in half. Remove yolks, reserving the whites. In a bowl, mash yolks. Stir in all remaining ingredients except paprika. Spoon or pipe into egg whites.
3. Refrigerate, covered, at least 30 minutes before serving. Sprinkle with paprika.

Party Deviled Eggs

Prep time: 10 minutes | Cook time: 5 minutes | Serves 4

1½ cups water
6 large eggs
⅛ cup mayonnaise
⅛ cup mustard
1 teaspoon white vinegar
⅛ teaspoon salt
⅛ teaspoon black pepper
¼ teaspoon paprika

1. Pour water into Instant Pot®. Place a trivet inside Instant Pot® and arrange eggs on top of trivet.
2. Close lid and set pressure release to Sealing.
3. Press Manual or Pressure Cook button and adjust time to 5 minutes.
4. When the timer beeps, allow pressure to release naturally for 5 minutes and then quick release remaining pressure. Unlock lid and remove it.
5. Carefully place eggs into a bowl of ice water. Leave eggs in ice bath 5 minutes. Remove eggs and peel.
6. Slice eggs in half and carefully scoop out yolk with a spoon. Place all yolks in a small bowl.
7. Add mayonnaise, mustard, vinegar, salt, and pepper to bowl of yolks. Mix until fully combined.
8. Scoop heaping spoonfuls of egg yolk mixture into center of halved hard-boiled eggs.
9. Sprinkle paprika on top of each deviled egg.
10. Chill eggs up to 24 hours until ready to be served.

Eggs, Raisins and Chorizo

Prep time: 5 minutes | Cook time: 13 minutes | Serves 3

1 tablespoon olive oil
⅓ cup onions, chopped
¼ pounds Mexican chorizo sausage, chopped
3 tablespoon raisins, soaked in water then drained
6 eggs
Salt and pepper, to taste

1. Press the Sauté button on the Instant Pot.
2. Heat the oil and sauté the onions until fragrant.
3. Add in the chorizo sausages and continue stirring for 3 minutes.
4. Stir in the raisins and eggs
5. Season with salt and pepper to taste.
6. Close the lid and press the Manual button.
7. Adjust the cooking time to 10 minutes.
8. Do natural pressure release.

Soft-Boiled Egg

Prep time: 5 minutes | Cook time: 3 minutes | Makes 1 or more large eggs

1 cup water, for steaming
1 or more large eggs

1. Place the eggs in the inner cooking pot. Pour the water into the inner cooking pot and place a trivet on the bottom. Place the eggs on the trivet. It's okay if they touch, and you can even stack them.
2. Pressure cook the eggs. Lock the lid into place and turn the valve to "sealing." Select Manual or Pressure Cook and adjust the pressure to High. Set the time for 3 minutes. When cooking ends, let the pressure release naturally for 3 minutes, then turn the valve to "venting" to quick release the remaining pressure.
3. Prepare the ice bath. While the eggs cook, fill a large bowl with ice and cold water.
4. Cool the eggs. Unlock and remove the lid. With a slotted spoon, transfer the eggs to the ice bath. This will stop the cooking. Allow the eggs to rest in the ice bath for 5 minutes.
5. Finish the eggs. Once the eggs have cooled, you can peel and eat them immediately, or store them whole in the refrigerator. Hard-boiled eggs will keep for up to 4 days. Soft-boiled eggs will keep for up to 2 days.

Steamed Beef Scotch Eggs

Prep time: 5 minutes | Cook time: 12 minutes | Serves 4

4 large eggs
1 pound (454 g) ground beef
1 tablespoon vegetable oil

1. Place a steamer basket in the Instant Pot and add a cup of water.
2. Place the eggs in the steamer basket and close the lid. Press the Steam button and adjust the cooking time to 6 minutes.
3. Once the timer beeps, do natural pressure release and take the eggs out. Place the eggs in an ice bath to arrest the cooking process.
4. When the eggs are cool, remove the shells. Set aside.
5. Divide the ground beef into four and flatten using your hands. Place the boiled egg in the middle and cover the entire egg with the ground beef. Do the same thing on the rest of the eggs. Set aside.
6. Press the Sauté button on the Instant Pot and add the oil. Once the oil is hot, brown the Scotch eggs on four sides. Set aside.
7. Place a steam rack in the Instant Pot and pour in a cup of water. Place the browned scotch eggs on the steamer rack and close the lid.
8. Press the Manual button and adjust the cooking time to 6 minutes.
9. Do natural pressure release.

Eggs and Veggie in Marinara Sauce

Prep time: 10 minutes | Cook time: 13 minutes | Serves 6

1 tablespoon coconut oil
2 cloves of garlic, minced
½ onion, diced
1 red bell pepper, diced
1 teaspoon chili powder
½ teaspoon paprika
½ teaspoon ground cumin
Salt and pepper, to taste
1½ cups Whole30-compliant marinara sauce
6 eggs
Parsley leaves, for garnish

1. Press the Sauté button on the Instant Pot.
2. Sauté the garlic and onions until fragrant.
3. Add the bell pepper, chili powder, paprika, and cumin. Season with salt and pepper to taste.
4. Continue stirring for 3 minutes.
5. Pour in the marinara sauce.
6. Gently crack the eggs into the marinara sauce.
7. Close the lid.
8. Press the Manual button and adjust the cooking time to 10 minutes.
9. Do natural pressure release.
10. Once the lid is opened, garnish with parsley.

Egg Pepper Cups with Mayo-Dijon Sauce

Prep time: 10 minutes | Cook time: 3 minutes | Serves 8

4 large eggs
4 medium bell peppers, tops and seeds removed
6 baby arugula leaves
Sauce:
¼ cup mayonnaise
1 teaspoon Dijon mustard
½ teaspoon lemon juice
½ teaspoon white vinegar
¼ teaspoon fine grind sea salt
⅛ teaspoon ground black pepper
¼ teaspoon ground turmeric

1. Place the trivet in the inner pot and add 1 cup water to the bottom of the pot. Make the sauce by combining the mayonnaise, Dijon mustard, lemon juice, vinegar, sea salt, black pepper, and turmeric in a small bowl.
2. Whisk until blended. Cover and refrigerate. Carefully crack 1 egg into each bell pepper cup, making sure to keep the yolk intact, and cover the top of each pepper with a small square of aluminum foil.
3. Place the covered peppers on the trivet. Lock the lid. Select the Manual mode and set the cooking time for 3 minutes on High Pressure.
4. Once the timer goes off, perform a natural pressure release for 2 minutes, then release any remaining pressure.
5. Carefully open the lid. Transfer the peppers to a serving platter. Remove the foil and top each pepper with 1 tablespoon of the sauce, and then garnish with the arugula leaves. Serve hot.

Eggs in Purgatory

Prep time: 5 minutes | Cook time: 15 minutes | Serves 4

2 tablespoons extra-virgin olive oil
1 small eggplant, cut into ½-inch pieces
3 large garlic cloves, minced
1 (28-ounce) can diced tomatoes, with most
    of the liquid drained out
1 tablespoon harissa or 1 teaspoon smoked
    paprika
¼ teaspoon red pepper flakes
½ teaspoon sea salt
¼ teaspoon freshly ground black pepper
4 to 6 eggs
1 tablespoon chopped fresh parsley
    (optional)
Hot sauce (optional)

1. Select Sauté on the Instant Pot. Heat the oil until it shimmers.
2. Sauté the eggplant until it starts to soften, about 4 minutes. Add the garlic and cook for 1 minute more.
3. Add the tomatoes, harissa, red pepper flakes, salt, and black pepper.
4. Secure the lid and seal the vent. Select Pressure Cook or Manual and cook on high pressure for 10 minutes, then quick release the pressure in the pot. Press Cancel and remove the lid.
5. Select Sauté and stir the sauce. Into a small bowl, crack one egg at a time. Lower each egg into the pot and gently pour it out of the bowl onto the sauce.
6. Simmer until the eggs are set but the yolks are runny, 4 to 6 minutes. Covering with a lid will speed up the process.
7. Top with the parsley and hot sauce (if using).

Bacon and Eggs

Prep time: 5 minutes | Cook time: 25 minutes | Serves 4

1 tablespoon coconut oil or ghee
6 slices bacon, diced
6 large eggs
¼ cup full-fat coconut milk
¼ cup nutritional yeast
¼ teaspoon sea salt
¼ teaspoon freshly ground black pepper
2 cups fresh kale leaves, chopped

1. Grease the bottom and sides of a 6- or 7-inch heatproof dish that fits inside the bowl of your Instant Pot with the ghee. Set aside.
2. Select Sauté on the Instant Pot. Cook the bacon until crispy, 5 to 8 minutes.
3. Meanwhile, in a medium bowl, whisk the eggs with the coconut milk, nutritional yeast, salt, and pepper. Set aside.
4. Stir the kale into the bacon. Press Cancel.
5. Pour the egg mixture into the prepared baking dish and, using a slotted spoon, add the bacon and kale. Cover with foil.
6. Place a trivet into the bowl and add 1½ cups of water. Place the dish containing the egg mixture onto the trivet.
7. Secure the lid and seal the vent. Select Pressure Cook or Manual and cook on high pressure for 20 minutes, then quick release the pressure in the pot and remove the lid. Depending on the depth of your dish, you may need an additional 5 or more minutes of cook time.
8. Remove the egg bake from the Instant Pot. Cut into pieces and serve.

Chapter 5 Basics

Pork Bone Broth

Prep time: 15 minutes | Cook time: 2 hours | Serves 8

4 pounds (1.8 kg) pork neck bones with meat
8 cups water
2 ribs celery, chopped in half
2 carrots, peeled and chopped in half
1 medium yellow onion, skin-on, quartered

5 cloves garlic, smashed
1 tablespoon apple cider vinegar
10 whole black peppercorns
1 teaspoon kosher salt
1 teaspoon poultry seasoning

2 sprigs thyme
2 sprigs rosemary
2 bay leaves
Any other seasonings you enjoy, to taste

1. Place the bones in the Instant Pot along with all the other ingredients. Stir well.
2. Secure the lid, move the valve to the sealing position, and hit Manual or Pressure Cook on High Pressure for 120 minutes. When done, allow a 30-minute natural release followed by a quick release. Allow to cool for 15 minutes.
3. Carefully pour the broth through a fine-mesh strainer with a large bowl or pot below it and discard all the solids. Now, taste the broth and season as you wish! The broth will keep in an airtight container or mason jar in the fridge for up to a week, and frozen for up to three months.

Chicken Bone Broth

Prep time: 15 minutes | Cook time: 1 hour 40 minutes | Makes 8 cups

Carcass from a roasted (3- to 4-pound / 1.4- to 1.8-kg) chicken
2 carrots, roughly chopped
3 stalks celery, roughly chopped
2 onions, roughly chopped
5 or 6 sprigs fresh parsley
1 sprig fresh thyme
2 tablespoons cider vinegar
10 whole black peppercorns
1 teaspoon salt

1. In an Instant Pot, place the carcass, carrots, celery, onions, parsley, thyme, vinegar, peppercorns, and salt. Add enough water to reach 1 inch below the maximum fill line. Lock the lid in place.
2. Select Soup/Broth. Use natural release.
3. Strain the broth through a fine-mesh strainer set over a large bowl or clean pot. Discard the solids. Transfer the broth to multiple containers to speed up cooling, don't freeze or refrigerate it while it's hot! Allow the broth to sit in the fridge, uncovered, for several hours, until the fat rises to the top and hardens. Scrape off the fat with a spoon and discard it.
4. Refrigerate the broth in airtight containers for 3 to 4 days or freeze for up to 6 months.

Beef Bone Broth

Prep time: 10 minutes | Cook time: 2½ hours | Makes 9 cups

3 to 4 pounds (1.4- to 1.8-kg) beef bones
2 carrots, roughly chopped
3 stalks celery, roughly chopped
2 onions, roughly chopped
5 or 6 fresh sprigs parsley
1 sprig fresh thyme
2 tablespoons cider vinegar
10 whole black peppercorns
1 teaspoon salt

1. Preheat the oven to 400°F (205°C). Place the bones in a shallow roasting pan or rimmed baking sheet. Roast until the bones are golden-brown, about 35 minutes.
2. In an Instant Pot, place the bones, carrots, celery, onions, parsley, thyme, vinegar, peppercorns, and salt. Add enough water to reach 1 inch below the maximum fill line. Lock the lid in place.
3. Select Manual and adjust to high pressure for 120 minutes. Use natural release.
4. Strain the broth through a fine-mesh strainer set over a large bowl or clean pot. Discard the solids. Transfer the broth to multiple containers to speed up cooling, don't freeze or refrigerate it while it's hot! Allow the broth sit in the fridge, uncovered, for several hours, until the fat rises to the top and hardens. Scrape off the fat with a spoon and discard it.
5. Refrigerate the broth in airtight containers for 3 to 4 days or freeze for up to 6 months.

Cinnamon Apple Sauce

Prep time: 5 minutes | Cook time: 10 minutes | Makes 6 cups

3 pounds (1.4 kg) apples (such as Fuji or McIntosh), peeled and sliced
½ teaspoon ground cinnamon
½ cup water

1. Add the apples, cinnamon, and water to the Instant Pot and secure the lid. Move the steam release valve to Sealing and select Manual/Pressure Cook to cook on high pressure for 10 minutes.
2. Let the pressure naturally release for 10 minutes, then move the steam release valve to Venting. When the floating valve drops, remove the lid.
3. Use a potato masher or immersion blender to puree the apples to the consistency of your choice. Serve the applesauce warm, or transfer it to an airtight container and chill in the fridge until ready to serve. Store the applesauce in the fridge for 1 week or in the freezer for 3 months.

Cauliflower Rice

Prep time: 5 minutes | Cook time: 1 minute | Serves 4

1 head cauliflower, cut into florets
Fine sea salt, to taste

1. Pour 1 cup water into the Instant Pot and arrange a steamer basket on the bottom. Place the cauliflower florets into the steamer basket, making sure that none of the cauliflower touches the water.
2. Secure the lid and move the steam release valve to Sealing. Select Manual/Pressure Cook to cook on high pressure for 1 minute. When the cooking cycle is complete, immediately move the steam release valve to Venting to quickly release the steam pressure. This ensures the cauliflower doesn't overcook. When the floating valve drops, press Cancel and remove the lid.
3. Use oven mitts to lift the steam basket out of the pot and pour out any water from the pot. Add the cooked cauliflower back to the pot. Season generously with salt and use a potato masher to break up the cauliflower into a ricelike consistency. Serve warm. Store leftovers in an airtight container in the fridge for 5 days.

White Mushroom Gravy

Prep time: 10 minutes | Cook time: 25 minutes | Makes 3 cups

3 tablespoons ghee or avocado oil
2 yellow onions, sliced
8 ounces (227 g) white or cremini mushrooms, cleaned and halved
3 cloves garlic, chopped
1½ teaspoons chopped fresh sage
1½ teaspoons chopped fresh thyme
1 teaspoon sea salt
2 pieces precooked organic bacon (optional)
3 cups chicken or vegetable stock, or bone broth

1. Place your healthy fat of choice in the Instant Pot and press sauté. Once the fat has melted, add the onions and sauté, stirring occasionally, for 5 minutes. Add the mushrooms and continue to sauté, stirring occasionally, for 7 minutes, or until the onions and mushrooms are light golden brown and caramelized. Add the garlic and sauté, stirring with a wooden spoon, for 1 minute or until fragrant, making sure to scrape up any browned bits at the bottom of the pot. Press keep warm/cancel and add the sage, thyme, salt, bacon (if using) and stock.
2. Secure the lid with the steam vent in the sealed position. Press manual and set on high pressure for 3 minutes.
3. Once the timer sounds, press keep warm/cancel. Using an oven mitt, do a quick release. When the steam venting stops and the silver dial drops, carefully open the lid.
4. Carefully transfer the hot gravy into a blender, making sure to leave at least 3 inches of headspace as hot liquids expand in the blender. Cover with the blender lid and, wearing an oven mitt while holding the lid closed, blend on low speed until completely pureed, about 30 seconds.
5. Transfer the gravy back into the Instant Pot, then press sauté and allow the gravy to simmer for 10 minutes to thicken. Once thickened, allow the gravy to sit and rest in the Instant Pot for about 15 minutes before serving.
6. Once the gravy has rested, it can be served immediately or stored for later use in an airtight glass container, such as a Mason jar, for up to 3 days.

Spaghetti Squash Noodles

Prep time: 5 minutes | Cook time: 8 minutes | Serves 4

1 (2- to 3-pound / 0.9- to 1.4-kg) medium-size spaghetti squash

1. Using a sharp knife, first trim off a small slice from each end of the spaghetti squash and discard.
2. Next, cut the spaghetti squash in half crosswise. Using a sharp spoon (I use an ice cream scoop) scoop out the seeds and stringy bits from the center of each cavity and discard.
3. Place the steamer insert into your Instant Pot and add 1 cup of water. Place the squash halves on top of the steamer insert, cut side up.
4. Close the lid on the Instant Pot and make sure the valve is sealed. Cook under high pressure for 8 minutes. When the cook time is complete, carefully turn the valve to rapidly release the pressure.
5. When the pressure has released, remove the lid from the pot. When cool enough to handle, tip the squash halves to pour out any collected liquid. Transfer cooked squash to a cutting board or plate and gently scrape out the strands that resemble spaghetti. Serve as desired.

Homemade Pumpkin Puree

Prep time: 5 minutes | Cook time: 10 minutes | Makes 2 to 3 cups

1 (2-pound / 907-g) pie pumpkin
1 cup water

1. Slice the pumpkin in half along its equator; remove the stem and seeds.
2. Pour the water into the Instant Pot and insert the steam trivet. Place the pumpkin, cut side down, on top of the trivet.
3. Secure the lid with the steam vent in the sealed position. Select manual or pressure, and cook on high pressure for 10 minutes.
4. Use a quick release, and make sure all the steam is released before taking off the lid. Using pot holders or tongs, carefully remove the pumpkin.
5. Gently scoop the flesh into a large bowl or food processor. Using an immersion blender or the food processor, pulse until smooth.
6. Store in the refrigerator for up to 1 week.

Caramelized Yellow Onion Compote

Prep time: 5 minutes | Cook time: 20 minutes | Makes 2 to 3 cups

3 tablespoons ghee
7 large yellow onions, thickly sliced
3 cloves garlic, minced
1 teaspoon sea salt
1 teaspoon finely chopped fresh thyme leaves
¼ cup filtered water

1. Place your healthy fat of choice in the Instant Pot and press sauté. Once the ghee has melted, add the onions, stirring occasionally for 7 minutes until the onions are light golden brown. Add the garlic, salt and thyme and sauté, stirring with a wooden spoon, for 1 minute, or until fragrant, making sure to scrape up any browned bits at the bottom of the pot. Press keep warm/cancel. Add the water and give it a quick stir.
2. Secure the lid with the steam vent in the sealed position. Press manual and set on high pressure for 7 minutes.
3. Once the timer sounds, press keep warm/cancel. Allow the Instant Pot to release pressure naturally for 5 minutes. Using an oven mitt, do a quick release. If there is any steam left over, allow it to release until the silver dial drops, then carefully open the lid.
4. Press sauté and, using a wooden spoon, stir occasionally for 5 minutes, or until all moisture has evaporated and the onions are a caramelized light brown color.
5. Use an immersion blender or transfer the onions to a food processor or high-powered blender and pulse just until they become a rustic mash, 5 to 7 seconds; do not overmix. You may need to do this in batches if you're using a blender.
6. Pour the onion compote into a serving dish or jar. Serve immediately as a condiment or serve slightly cooled off or at room temperature as a spread with appetizers.

Chapter 6 Poultry

Chicken with Barbecue Sauce

Prep time: 15 minutes | Cook time: 20 minutes | Serves 4

For the Barbecue Sauce:

3 pitted Medjool dates

½ cup hot water

1 (15-ounce / 425-g) can Whole30-compliant tomato sauce, preferably no salt added

½ cup cider vinegar

1 tablespoon smoked paprika

2 teaspoons Whole30-compliant brown mustard

2 teaspoons onion powder

1 teaspoon garlic powder

½ teaspoon salt (omit if tomato sauce contains salt)

For the Chicken:

1 tablespoon extra-virgin olive or avocado oil

1 medium red onion, sliced

2 cloves garlic, minced

1½ to 2 pounds (680- to 907-g) boneless, skinless chicken breasts or thighs

2 teaspoons Whole30-compliant BBQ rub

4 small sweet potatoes or white potatoes

2 green onions, thinly sliced

Make the Barbecue Sauce

1. Soak the dates in the hot water until softened, about 2 minutes. Place the dates and water in a food processor or high speed blender. Add the tomato sauce, vinegar, paprika, mustard, onion powder, garlic powder, and salt (if using). Cover and process or blend until smooth; set aside.

Make the Chicken

2. Select Sauté on a 6-quart Instant Pot and adjust to Normal/Medium. Add the olive oil to the pot. When it's hot, add the onion and cook, stirring, for 1 minute. Add the garlic and cook, stirring, until just softened, 30 to 60 seconds. Select Cancel. Season both sides of the chicken with the BBQ rub and add to the pot. Add 2 cups of the barbecue sauce and stir to combine. Lock the lid in place.

3. Select Manual and cook on high pressure for 12 minutes. Use quick release. Transfer the chicken to a plate; cover to keep warm. Select Sauté. Cook the sauce, stirring, until thickened, about 5 minutes. Select Cancel.

4. Meanwhile, prick the sweet potatoes all over with a fork. Microwave on high, turning once, until tender, 8 to 10 minutes. Use two forks to shred the chicken. Return the chicken to the pot and toss with the sauce. Slice the potatoes open. Serve the chicken over the potatoes and top with green onions.

Coconut Chicken Breast with Cauliflower Rice

Prep time: 15 minutes | Cook time: 19 minutes | Serves 4

4 tablespoons coconut oil

4 skinless, boneless chicken breast halves (1½-pound / 680-g total)

1 cup chopped cored fresh tomatoes

¼ cup Whole30-compliant chicken broth

1 to 2 pitted dates

1 tablespoon Whole30-compliant red curry paste

4 cloves garlic, minced

½ teaspoon ground ginger

½ teaspoon ground coriander

¾ teaspoon salt

¾ cup Whole30-compliant canned coconut milk

2 tablespoons clarified butter or ghee

1 (16-ounce / 454-g) package fresh cauliflower crumbles or 4 cups raw cauliflower crumbles

1 teaspoon cumin seeds, crushed

⅓ cup chopped fresh cilantro

¼ cup thinly sliced green onion tops

1. On a 6-quart Instant Pot, select Sauté and adjust to Normal/Medium. Add 1 tablespoon of the oil to the pot. When it's hot, add half the chicken. Cook, turning once, until browned, 4 to 6 minutes. Transfer the chicken to a bowl. Repeat with 1 tablespoon oil and the remaining chicken. Return all the chicken to the pot.
2. In a medium bowl, combine the tomatoes, broth, dates, curry paste, garlic, ginger, coriander, and ½ teaspoon of the salt. Add to the pot with the chicken. Lock the lid in place.
3. Select Manual and cook on high pressure for 4 minutes. Use quick release. Transfer the chicken to a cutting board and cut into bite-size pieces. Set aside.
4. Add the coconut milk and butter to the tomato mixture in the pot. Use an immersion blender to blend until smooth. (Or, transfer the tomato mixture to a regular blender; cover and blend until smooth.) Add the chicken to the sauce in the pot. Select Sauté and adjust to Normal/Medium. Cook, stirring occasionally, until slightly thickened, 3 to 5 minutes.
5. Meanwhile, in a large skillet, heat the remaining 2 tablespoons oil over medium heat. When it's hot, add the cauliflower, cumin seeds, and remaining ¼ teaspoon salt. Cook, stirring occasionally, until the cauliflower is crisp-tender and starting to brown, 4 to 6 minutes.
6. Serve the chicken and sauce on the cauliflower and sprinkle with the cilantro and green onion tops.

Indian Chicken Tikka Masala

Prep time: 20 minutes | Cook time: 30 minutes | Serves 4

2 pounds (907 g) boneless, skinless chicken breasts, cut into 1-inch cubes
¾ cup low-sodium chicken broth
2 cups diced yellow onion (1 large)
1 (6-ounce / 170-g) can tomato paste
2 tablespoons extra virgin olive oil
4 garlic cloves, minced
1 (1-inch) piece fresh ginger, finely grated
1 tablespoon curry powder
1½ teaspoons kosher salt
1 teaspoon freshly ground black pepper
1 teaspoon ground turmeric
1 teaspoon ground cumin
1 teaspoon paprika
½ teaspoon cayenne pepper (adjust according to your heat preference)
½ teaspoon ground cinnamon
1 bay leaf
1 (13-ounce / 368.5-g) can Whole30-compliant coconut milk (shaken to combine well)
2 tablespoons arrowroot starch
1 tablespoon fresh lemon juice (½ lemon)
Prepared Cauliflower Rice (optional)
¼ cup fresh cilantro leaves, for serving

1. Combine the chicken, broth, onion, tomato paste, olive oil, garlic, ginger, curry powder, salt, black pepper, turmeric, cumin, paprika, cayenne pepper, and cinnamon in the Instant Pot. Stir well. Place the bay leaf on top, cover and seal. Press the poultry button and increase time to 20 minutes.
2. When cook time is complete, release the pressure manually by carefully turning the valve and opening the Instant Pot. Discard the bay leaf. Turn on the sauté function. In a medium bowl, whisk together the coconut milk and arrowroot starch. Add the mixture to the Instant Pot with the cooked chicken and let simmer until the sauce has thickened, about 10 more minutes.

Jerk Chicken with Vegetable and Pineapple

Prep time: 10 minutes | Cook time: 9 minutes | Serves 4

½ cup Whole30-compliant chicken broth
2 medium red onions, cut into large wedges
2 red bell peppers, cut into 1-inch pieces
2 cups 1-inch cubes pineapple
1 jalapeño, seeded and chopped
¾ teaspoon salt
½ teaspoon ground allspice
½ teaspoon garlic powder
¼ teaspoon ground cinnamon
⅛ teaspoon cayenne pepper
4 boneless, skinless chicken breasts (1½-pound / 680-g)
1 (12-ounce / 340-g) package frozen riced cauliflower or 3 cups raw cauliflower rice (see page 60)
Chopped fresh cilantro (optional)

1. In a 6-quart Instant Pot, stir together the broth, onions, bell peppers, pineapple, and jalapeño.
2. In a small bowl, stir together the salt, allspice, garlic powder, cinnamon, and cayenne pepper. Sprinkle the chicken with the seasoning. Place the chicken in a single layer on top of the onion mixture. Lock the lid in place.
3. Select Manual and cook on high pressure for 9 minutes. Use quick release.
4. Meanwhile, prepare the cauliflower rice according to the package directions.
5. Serve the chicken and vegetables over the cauliflower rice; drizzle with some of the cooking juices. If desired, top with cilantro.

Buffalo Chicken Wings

Prep time: 5 minutes | Cook time: 15 minutes | Serves 4

2 pounds (907 g) frozen chicken
  wings
½ tablespoon Whole30-compliant
  Cajun seasoning
1½ cups water
1 cup Whole30-compliant buffalo
  wing sauce

1. In a large bowl, toss chicken wings in Cajun seasoning so they are evenly coated.
2. Pour water into Instant Pot® and add a trivet.
3. Place wings in a 7" springform pan. Create a foil sling and lower pan into Instant Pot®.
4. Close lid and set pressure release to Sealing.
5. Press Manual or Pressure Cook button and adjust time to 15 minutes.
6. When the timer beeps, allow pressure to release naturally and then unlock lid and remove it. Remove pan from Instant Pot® using foil sling.
7. Remove wings and brush with buffalo sauce. Serve hot.

Herb Chicken with Veggie-Almond Salad

Prep time: 15 minutes | Cook time: 30 minutes | Serves 4

For the Chicken:
¼ cup clarified butter or ghee
1½ teaspoons salt
1 teaspoon smoked paprika
1 teaspoon dried thyme
½ teaspoon dried rosemary
½ teaspoon garlic powder
½ teaspoon black pepper
1 (3- to 3½-pound / 1.4- to 1.6-kg) whole chicken, giblets removed
1 lemon, cut in half

For the Salad:
1 large fennel bulb, trimmed and very thinly sliced
3 stalks celery, very thinly sliced
¼ cup sliced almonds, toasted
¼ cup packed fresh flat-leaf parsley leaves
3 tablespoons extra-virgin olive oil
2 tablespoons fresh lemon juice
¼ teaspoon salt
⅛ to ¼ teaspoon black pepper

Make the Chicken
1. Place the rack in a 6-quart Instant Pot. Add 1½ cups water to the pot.
2. In a small bowl, combine the butter, salt, paprika, thyme, rosemary, garlic powder, and black pepper. Distribute half of the butter mixture under the skin of the chicken and rub the other half on the outside. Place the lemon halves in the cavity. Place the chicken, breast side up, on the rack. Lock the lid in place.
3. Select Manual and cook on high pressure for 30 minutes. Use natural release.

Make the Salad
4. Meanwhile, in a large bowl, combine the fennel, celery, almonds, parsley, olive oil, and lemon juice. Sprinkle with the salt and pepper; toss to combine.
5. Carefully transfer the chicken to a serving platter. Discard the cooking liquid. Serve the chicken with the salad.

Barbecue Chicken Wings

Prep time: 5 minutes | Cook time: 15 minutes | Serves 4

2 pounds (907 g) frozen chicken wings
½ tablespoon garlic salt
1½ cups water
1 cup Whole30-compliant barbecue sauce

1. In a large bowl, toss chicken wings in garlic salt so they are evenly coated.
2. Pour water into Instant Pot® and add a trivet.
3. Place wings in a 7" springform pan. Create a foil sling and lower pan into Instant Pot®.
4. Close lid and set pressure release to Sealing.
5. Press Manual or Pressure Cook button and adjust time to 15 minutes.
6. When the timer beeps, allow pressure to release naturally and then unlock lid and remove it. Remove pan from Instant Pot® using foil sling.
7. Remove wings and brush with barbecue sauce. Serve hot.

Hawaiian Chicken with Pineapple

Prep time: 5 minutes | Cook time: 15 minutes | Serves 4

1 pound (454 g) boneless, skinless chicken breasts
1 (20-ounce /567-g) can crushed pineapple
1 (18-ounce / 510-g) bottle Whole30-compliant barbecue sauce

1. Add chicken, pineapple (with juice), and barbecue sauce to the Instant Pot®. Stir to combine.
2. Close lid and set pressure release to Sealing.
3. Press Manual or Pressure Cook button and adjust time to 15 minutes.
4. When the timer beeps, allow pressure to release naturally and then unlock lid and remove it.
5. Serve.

Mexican Chicken Tinga

Prep time: 15 minutes | Cook time: 10 minutes | Serves 6

1 medium yellow onion, chopped
1 (14½-ounce / 411-g) can Whole30-compliant fire-roasted tomatoes, undrained
1 cup Whole30-compliant chicken broth
2 cloves garlic
1½ teaspoons chipotle powder
1 teaspoon dried oregano
1 teaspoon salt
½ teaspoon ground cumin
¼ teaspoon ground cinnamon
2½ pounds (1.1 kg) bone-in chicken thighs, skin removed (see Tip, page 169)
2 (12-ounce / 340-g) packages frozen riced cauliflower and sweet potato
1 avocado, halved, pitted, peeled, and sliced
1 lime, cut into wedges

1. For the sauce, in a blender, combine the onion, tomatoes, broth, garlic, chipotle powder, oregano, salt, cumin, and cinnamon. Cover and blend until smooth. Add the sauce to a 6-quart Instant Pot. Add the chicken to the sauce. Lock the lid in place.
2. Select Manual and cook on high pressure for 10 minutes. Use natural release.
3. Meanwhile, prepare the riced cauliflower and sweet potato according to the package directions.
4. Transfer the chicken to a plate; let cool slightly. Remove and discard the bones. Use two forks to shred the chicken. Return the chicken to the pot and stir to coat.
5. Serve the chicken and sauce in shallow bowls with the cauliflower–sweet potato mixture. Serve with the avocado slices and lime wedges.

Turkey Chili with Avocado and Cilantro

Prep time: 10 minutes | Cook time: 13 minutes | Serves 4

1 tablespoon extra-virgin olive oil
1 (19-ounce / 538.6-g) package lean ground turkey
1 large yellow onion, chopped
2 cloves garlic, minced
1 teaspoon salt
1 (28-ounce / 794-g) can Whole30-compliant crushed tomatoes
1 medium yellow bell pepper, chopped
1 medium jalapeño, seeded and chopped
1 tablespoon chili powder
1 medium avocado, halved, pitted, peeled, and diced
2 tablespoons chopped fresh cilantro

1. On a 6-quart Instant Pot, select Sauté and adjust to Normal/Medium. Add the oil to the pot. When it's hot, add the turkey, onion, garlic, and salt. Cook, stirring occasionally with a wooden spoon to break up the meat, until browned, 8 to 10 minutes. Select Cancel.
2. Stir in ½ cup water, the tomatoes, bell pepper, jalapeño, and chili powder. Lock the lid in place. Select Manual and cook on high pressure for 5 minutes. Use quick release.
3. Top servings with the avocado and cilantro.

Indian-Style Chicken Thighs

Prep time: 20 minutes | Cook time: 45 minutes | Serves 4

3 tablespoons clarified butter or ghee

1 large sweet onion, diced

1 piece (2 inches) fresh ginger, peeled and minced

3 cloves garlic, minced

2 bay leaves

8 boneless, skinless chicken thighs (2- to 2½-pound / 0.9- to 1.1-kg)

1 tablespoon Whole30-compliant garam masala

1½ tablespoons ground turmeric

1 tablespoon ground cumin

1 teaspoon fine sea salt

1½ teaspoons black pepper

2 tablespoons fresh lemon juice

1 teaspoon cider vinegar

1 cinnamon stick

1 cup Whole30-compliant coconut milk

1 tablespoon grass-fed beef gelatin

½ cup chopped almonds

1 (12-ounce / 340-g) package frozen riced cauliflower or 3 cups raw cauliflower rice

⅓ cup chopped fresh cilantro

1. On a 6-quart Instant Pot, select Sauté and adjust to Normal/Medium. Add the butter. When it's hot, add the onion, ginger, garlic, and bay leaves. Cook until the onion is tender, 5 to 6 minutes. Add the chicken, garam masala, turmeric, cumin, salt, and pepper and stir to combine. Cook, stirring occasionally, until the chicken is lightly browned, about 10 minutes. Add the lemon juice, vinegar, and cinnamon stick. Stir, scraping up any browned bits from the bottom of the pot. Stir in the coconut milk. Bring to a simmer. Select Cancel. Stir in the gelatin until dissolved. Lock the lid in place.
2. Select Manual and cook on high pressure for 20 minutes. Use quick release.
3. Select Sauté and adjust to Normal/Medium. Stir in the almonds. Simmer until the liquid is reduced by one-third, about 10 minutes.
4. Meanwhile, prepare the cauliflower rice.
5. Remove and discard the bay leaves and cinnamon stick. Serve the chicken mixture over the cauliflower and top with the cilantro.

Chinese Sesame Chicken Breast

Prep time: 15 minutes | Cook time: 12 minutes | Serves 4

2 pounds (907 g) boneless, skinless chicken breasts, sliced into thin strips

½ teaspoon black pepper

1 tablespoon plus 1 teaspoon arrowroot powder

3 tablespoons avocado oil

½ cup Whole30-compliant chicken broth

¼ cup coconut aminos

1 tablespoon rice vinegar

2 teaspoons toasted sesame oil

½ teaspoon Whole30-compliant fish sauce

¼ teaspoon red pepper flakes (optional)

1 (11-ounce / 311.8-g) package frozen broccoli florets, or 4 cups broccoli florets, steamed

2 tablespoons sesame seeds, toasted

2 green onions, sliced

1. Place the chicken in a medium bowl and sprinkle with the pepper. Add 1 tablespoon of the arrowroot and toss to coat.
2. On a 6-quart Instant Pot, select Sauté and adjust to Normal/Medium. Add the avocado oil. When it's hot, add half the chicken and cook, stirring once, until golden brown, about 6 minutes. Transfer to a plate. Repeat with the remaining chicken. Select Cancel.
3. Meanwhile, in a small bowl, whisk together the broth, coconut aminos, vinegar, sesame oil, fish sauce, and remaining 1 teaspoon arrowroot until the arrowroot is dissolved. Add red pepper flakes (if using).
4. Return all of the chicken to the pot. Pour the sauce over the chicken. Lock the lid in place. Select Manual and cook for 6 minutes. Use quick release. Stir the chicken. Let stand until slightly thickened, 5 to 10 minutes. Meanwhile, cook the broccoli according to package directions.
5. Serve the chicken over the broccoli. Sprinkle with the sesame seeds and green onions.

Garlicky Chicken

Prep time: 10 minutes | Cook time: 24 minutes | Serves 4

3 to 3½ pounds (1.4- to 1.6-kg) meaty chicken pieces (breast halves, drumsticks, and thighs)
½ teaspoon salt
1 tablespoon clarified butter, ghee, or other Whole30-compliant fat
40 cloves garlic (about 2 heads), peeled
2 teaspoons Whole30-compliant Italian seasoning
1 cup Whole30-compliant chicken broth
2 sprigs fresh rosemary (optional)
2 sprigs fresh thyme (optional)
1 (5-ounce / 142-g) package mixed salad greens (optional)
Whole30-compliant Italian dressing (optional)

1. Sprinkle the chicken with the salt. On a 6-quart Instant Pot, select Sauté and adjust to Normal/Medium. Add the butter. When it's melted, add half the chicken, skin sides down, and cook, turning once, until browned on both sides, about 8 minutes. Transfer to a plate. Repeat with the remaining chicken.
2. Add the garlic to the pot. Cook, stirring frequently, 1 to 2 minutes. Add half the chicken and season with half the Italian seasoning. Repeat with the remaining chicken and seasoning. Add the broth. Lock the lid in place.
3. Select Manual and cook on high pressure for 15 minutes. Use natural release for 10 minutes, then quick release.
4. Serve the garlic with the chicken. If desired, top with fresh rosemary and thyme, and serve with greens drizzled with dressing.

✕ Shredded Chicken Breast

Prep time: 5 minutes | Cook time: 15 minutes | Serves 4

1 pound (454 g) boneless, skinless chicken breasts
1½ cups chicken broth
1 teaspoon salt
¼ teaspoon black pepper

1. Place chicken, broth, salt, and pepper into Instant Pot®.
2. Close lid and set pressure release to Sealing.
3. Press Manual or Pressure Cook button and adjust time to 15 minutes.
4. When the timer beeps, allow pressure to release naturally and then unlock lid and remove it.
5. Remove chicken from Instant Pot® and shred with two forks. Use in any recipe calling for cooked chicken.

Chicken with Tomato

Prep time: 10 minutes | Cook time: 20 minutes | Serves 4

1 can crushed tomatoes
6 cloves of garlic
2 teaspoons ginger, grated
1 teaspoon turmeric
½ teaspoon cayenne pepper
1 teaspoon paprika
1 teaspoon garam masala
1 teaspoon cumin
1 pound (454 g) chicken meat

1. Put everything in the Instant Pot.
2. Close the lid and press the Poultry button.
3. Adjust the cooking time to 20 minutes.
4. Do natural pressure release.

Italian Chicken with Potatoes

Prep time: 10 minutes | Cook time: 15 minutes | Serves 8

2 pounds (907 g) chicken
1 cup Whole30-compliant BBQ sauce
½ cup water
1 tablespoon Italian seasoning
1 tablespoon minced garlic
3 large potatoes, peeled and chopped
1 large onion, sliced

1. Place all ingredients in the Instant Pot.
2. Give a good stir.
3. Close the lid and press the Poultry button.
4. Adjust the cooking time to 15 minutes.
5. Do quick pressure release.

Spiced Whole Chicken

Prep time: 5 minutes | Cook time: 40 minutes | Serves 6

1 (6-pound / 2.7-kg) whole chicken
1 teaspoon salt
½ teaspoon black pepper
½ teaspoon paprika
½ teaspoon garlic powder
1 tablespoon olive oil
1 cup water

1. Remove giblets from chicken and discard giblets.
2. In a small bowl, mix together salt, pepper, paprika, and garlic powder. Rub spice mixture on chicken.
3. Press Sauté button and pour oil into Instant Pot®.
4. Add chicken and brown both sides of chicken in Instant Pot®, about 1 minute per side. Turn off Instant Pot® and remove chicken.
5. Pour water into Instant Pot® and add trivet. Place chicken on top of trivet.
6. Close lid and set pressure release to Sealing.
7. Press Manual or Pressure Cook button and adjust time to 38 minutes.
8. When the timer beeps, allow pressure to release naturally and then unlock lid and remove it.
9. Serve chicken hot or cold.

Barbecue Chicken and Smoked Sausage

Prep time: 10 minutes | Cook time: 24 minutes | Serves 8

1 medium onion, chopped
1 large sweet red pepper, cut into 1-in. pieces
4 bone-in chicken thighs, skin removed
4 chicken drumsticks, skin removed
1 (12-ounce / 340-g) package smoked sausage
   links, cut into 1-in. pieces
1 cup chicken broth
1 cup Whole30-compliant barbecue sauce
Sliced seeded jalapeno pepper, optional

1. Place first six ingredients in a 6-qt. electric pressure cooker; top with barbecue sauce. Lock lid; make sure vent is closed. Select manual setting; adjust pressure to high, and set time for 12 minutes. When finished cooking, quick-release pressure according to manufacturer's directions (a thermometer inserted in chicken should read at least 170°). Remove chicken, sausage and vegetables from cooker; keep warm.
2. Select saute setting and adjust for high heat; bring liquid to a boil. Reduce heat; simmer until thickened, 12-15 minutes, stirring occasionally.
3. Serve chicken, sausage and vegetables with sauce. If desired, top with jalapeno.

Classic Chicken Cacciatore

Prep time: 10 minutes | Cook time: 15 minutes | Serves 6

2 medium onions, thinly sliced
1 (3- to 4-pound / 1.4- to 1.8-kg) broiler/fryer chicken,
   cut up and skin removed
2 garlic cloves, minced
1 to 2 teaspoons dried oregano
1 teaspoon salt
½ teaspoon dried basil
¼ teaspoon pepper
1 bay leaf
1 (14½-ounce / 411-g) can diced tomatoes, undrained
1 (8-ounce / 227-g) can tomato sauce
1 (4-ounce / 113-g) can mushroom stems and pieces, drained
¼ cup water

1. Place onions in a 6-qt. electric pressure cooker. Add the next 11 ingredients. Lock lid; make sure vent is closed. Select manual setting; adjust pressure to high and set time for 15 minutes.
2. When finished cooking, allow pressure to naturally release for 10 minutes, then quick-release any remaining pressure according to manufacturer's directions. Discard bay leaf. Serve chicken with sauce.

Chicken Cacciatore with Zoodles

Prep time: 15 minutes | Cook time: 22 minutes | Serves 4

8 boneless, skinless chicken thighs (about 2¼-pound / 1.0-kg)
1 teaspoon dried oregano
1 teaspoon salt
¼ teaspoon black pepper
1 tablespoon coconut oil
1 medium onion, chopped
1 red bell pepper, cut into 1-inch pieces
1 (8-ounce / 227-g) package sliced mushrooms
1 (14½-ounce / 411-g) can Whole30-compliant diced tomatoes, undrained
½ cup Whole30-compliant chicken broth
2 tablespoons Whole30-compliant tomato paste
2 cloves garlic, minced
1 (10½-ounce / 298-g) package zucchini noodles or 2 small zucchini, spiralized
Fresh chopped parsley (optional)

1. Season the chicken with the oregano, ½ teaspoon of the salt, and the pepper. Add the coconut oil to a 6-quart Instant Pot. Select Sauté and adjust to Normal/Medium. When the oil is hot, add half of the chicken and cook, turning once, until browned on both sides, 4 to 8 minutes. Repeat with the remaining chicken. Select Cancel. Transfer the chicken to a plate.
2. Add the onion, bell pepper, mushrooms, tomatoes, broth, tomato paste, garlic, and remaining ½ teaspoon salt to the pot. Add the chicken. Lock the lid in place.
3. Select Manual and cook on high pressure for 12 minutes. Use quick release.
4. Transfer the chicken to a plate; cover to keep warm. Select Sauté and adjust to Normal/Medium. When the sauce is simmering, add the zucchini noodles. Cook, stirring frequently, until the sauce is thickened and the zucchini is crisp-tender, about 2 minutes. Select Cancel. Serve, topped with parsley if desired.

Turkey with Apple and Berry Compote

Prep time: 10 minutes | Cook time: 45 minutes | Serves 12

1 teaspoon salt
½ teaspoon garlic powder
½ teaspoon dried thyme
½ teaspoon pepper
2 boneless skinless turkey breast halves (2-pound / 907-g each)
⅓ cup water

For the Compote:
2 medium apples, peeled and finely chopped
2 cups fresh raspberries
2 cups fresh blueberries
1 cup white grape juice
¼ teaspoon crushed red pepper flakes
¼ teaspoon ground ginger

1. Mix salt, garlic powder, thyme and pepper; rub over turkey breasts. Place in a 6-qt. electric pressure cooker. Pour water around turkey. Lock lid; make sure vent is closed. Select manual setting; adjust pressure to high and set time for 30 minutes. When finished cooking, allow pressure to naturally release for 10 minutes, then quick-release any remaining pressure according to manufacturer's directions. A thermometer inserted in turkey breasts should read at least 165°F (74°C).
2. Carefully remove turkey and cooking juices from pressure cooker; tent with foil. Let stand before slicing while you prepare the compote.
3. In pressure cooker, select saute setting, and adjust for high heat. Add compote ingredients. Bring to a boil. Reduce the heat to medium; cook, uncovered, stirring occasionally, until slightly thickened and apples are tender, 15-20 minutes. Serve turkey with compote.

✕ Western Chicken with Vegetables

Prep time: 15 minutes | Cook time: 12 minutes | Serves 4

2 tablespoons olive oil
1 pound (454 g) chicken thighs
Salt and black pepper, to taste
½ pound (227 g) asparagus, stems removed
2 large carrots, chopped
½ pound (227 g) baby russet potatoes, quartered
½ pound (227 g) radishes, halved
2 cups chicken broth
2 tablespoons smoked paprika
1 teaspoon garlic powder
1 teaspoon onion powder
3 fresh rosemary sprigs

1. Set to Sauté, heat olive oil, season chicken with salt and pepper, and fry until golden brown on both sides, 6 minutes; set aside. Sweat asparagus and carrots for 1 minute, and add potatoes, radishes, broth, paprika, garlic powder, onion powder, rosemary sprigs, and chicken. Seal the lid, select Manual/Pressure Cook on High, and set time to 4 minutes.
2. After cooking, do a natural pressure release for 10 minutes. Unlock the lid, discard rosemary sprigs, stir, and adjust the taste. Spoon chicken and vegetables onto serving plates; set aside. Select Sauté and cook the remaining sauce until reduced and thickened, 2 minutes. Drizzle sauce over chicken and vegetables and serve warm.

Turkey Breast and Pomegranate Seeds

Prep time: 10 minutes | Cook time: 25 minutes | Serves 4

1 big turkey breast, skinless, boneless and sliced
1 cup pomegranate seeds
1 cup chicken stock
1 tablespoon sweet paprika
1 tablespoon olive oil
A pinch of salt and black pepper
1 tablespoon cilantro, chopped

1. Set the instant pot on Sauté mode, add the oil, heat it up, add the meat and brown for 5 minutes.
2. Add the rest of the ingredients, put the lid on and cook on High for 25 minutes.
3. Release the pressure naturally for 10 minutes, divide everything between plates and serve.

✕ Simple Chicken Breast

Prep time: 5 minutes | Cook time: 30 minutes | Serves 8

4 pounds (1.8 kg) chicken breasts
½ cup water
Salt and pepper, to taste

1. Place all ingredients in the Instant Pot.
2. Close the lid and press the Poultry button.
3. Adjust the cooking time to 30 minutes.
4. Do natural pressure release.
5. Use two forks to shred the chicken meat. Remove bones if any.

Sauté Turkey and Cauliflower

Prep time: 10 minutes | Cook time: 35 minutes | Serves 4

1 yellow onion, chopped
2 pounds (907 g) turkey breast, skinless, boneless and sliced
1 cup cauliflower florets
1 cup chicken stock
2 tablespoons olive oil
2 garlic cloves, minced
A pinch of rosemary, dried
A pinch of salt and black pepper

1. Set your instant pot on Sauté mode, add the oil, heat it up, add the onion, cauliflower, garlic, rosemary, salt and pepper, toss and sauté for 10 minutes.
2. Add the turkey and the stock, put the lid on and cook on High for 25 minutes.
3. Release the pressure naturally for 10 minutes, divide the mix between plates and serve.

Chicken Breast and Cayenne Tomatoes

Prep time: 10 minutes | Cook time: 20 minutes | Serves 4

1½ pounds (680 g) chicken breast, skinless, boneless and cubed
1 cup tomatoes, cubed
1 tablespoon avocado oil
A pinch of salt and black pepper
1 teaspoon cayenne pepper
1 cup chicken stock
1 tablespoon smoked paprika
1 tablespoon cilantro, chopped

1. Set your instant pot on Sauté mode, add the oil, heat it up, add the meat and brown for 2 to 3 minutes.
2. Add the rest of the ingredients, put the lid on and cook on High for 18 minutes.
3. Release the pressure naturally for 10 minutes, divide everything between plates and serve.

Chicken Breast, Tomato and Bell Peppers

Prep time: 10 minutes | Cook time: 25 minutes | Serves 4

2 chicken breasts, skinless, boneless and cubed
2 tablespoons olive oil
1 teaspoon Creole seasoning
A pinch of cayenne pepper
1 cup tomato, cubed
1 cup mixed bell peppers, cubed
1 yellow onion, chopped
1 cup chicken stock

1. Set the instant pot on Sauté mode, add the oil, heat it up, add the onion and the chicken and brown for 5 minutes.
2. Add the other ingredients, put the lid on and cook on High for 20 minutes.
3. Release the pressure naturally for 10 minutes, divide everything between plates and serve.

Chicken Breast, Bacon and Artichokes

Prep time: 10 minutes | Cook time: 25 minutes | Serves 4

1 cup Whole30-compliant bacon, cooked and crumbled
2 chicken breasts, skinless, boneless and halved
2 cups canned artichokes, drained and chopped
1 cup Whole30-compliant chicken stock
1 tablespoon chives, chopped
2 tablespoons tomato paste

1. In your instant pot, mix the chicken with the rest of the ingredients, put the lid on and cook on High for 25 minutes.
2. Release the pressure naturally for 10 minutes, divide everything between plates and serve.

Whole Chicken with Spice Rub

Prep time: 10 minutes | Cook time: 40 minutes | Serves 6

1 whole chicken
1½ teaspoons salt
½ teaspoon pepper
1 teaspoon minced garlic
1 teaspoon paprika
1¾ tablespoons olive oil
1 cup chicken broth

1. In a mixing bowl, mix all ingredients except for the chicken broth.
2. Make sure to massage the chicken until all surfaces are covered by the spice rub.
3. Pour the chicken broth into the Instant Pot.
4. Add the chicken.
5. Close the lid and press the Poultry button.
6. Adjust the cooking time to 40 minutes.
7. Do natural pressure release.

Cuban Mojo Chicken

Prep time: 10 minutes | Cook time: 15 minutes | Serves 12

¼ cup olive oil
12 chicken breasts, skin and bones removed
8 cloves of garlic, minced
⅔ cup lime juice, freshly squeezed
⅔ cup orange juice, freshly squeezed
1 tablespoon orange peel
1 tablespoon dried oregano
2 tablespoons ground cumin
Salt and pepper, to taste
¼ cup cilantro, chopped

1. Press the Sauté button on the Instant Pot.
2. Stir in the chicken breasts and garlic. Cook until the chicken pieces have turned lightly brown.
3. Add the rest of the ingredients except for the cilantro.
4. Close the lid and press the Poultry button.
5. Adjust the cooking time to 15 minutes.
6. Do quick pressure release.
7. Garnish with cilantro.

Pomegranate and Cranbreey Turkey Breast

Prep time: 10 minutes | Cook time: 30 minutes | Serves 4

2 tablespoons avocado oil
1 big turkey breast, skinless, boneless and sliced
A pinch of salt and black pepper
1 cup cranberries
1 cup pomegranate juice
1 cup walnuts, chopped
1 bunch thyme, chopped

1. Set your instant pot on sauté mode, add the oil, heat it up, add the meat and brown for 5 minutes.
2. Add the rest of the ingredients, put the lid on and cook on High for 25 minutes.
3. Release the pressure naturally for 10 minutes, divide everything between plates and serve.

Tangy Turkey Wings

Prep time: 10 minutes | Cook time: 30 minutes | Serves 4

1 yellow onion, chopped
2 turkey wings, halved
1 tablespoon avocado oil
2 tablespoons lime juice
1 tablespoon lime zest, grated
4 garlic cloves, minced
1 cup chicken stock
A pinch of salt and black pepper

1. Set your instant pot on sauté mode, add the oil, heat it up, add the onion and sauté for 2 minutes.
2. Add the turkey and the rest of the ingredients, put the lid on and cook on High for 28 minutes.
3. Release the pressure naturally for 10 minutes, divide everything between plates and serve.

Chicken Wings and Tomato-Scallions Sauce

Prep time: 10 minutes | Cook time: 25 minutes | Serves 4

8 chicken wings
A pinch of salt and black pepper
1 tablespoon olive oil
6 scallions, chopped
½ teaspoon garlic powder
1 tomato, chopped
¼ cup cilantro, chopped
2 cups chicken stock
8 ounces Whole30-compliant tomato sauce

1. Set your instant pot on Sauté mode, add the oil, heat it up, add the scallions, garlic powder, salt and pepper and sauté for 5 minutes.
2. Add the chicken wings and brown for 5 minutes more.
3. Add the remaining ingredients, put the lid on and cook on High for 15 minutes.
4. Release the pressure naturally for 10 minutes, divide everything between plates and serve.

Smoked Paprika Turkey Breast

Prep time: 5 minutes | Cook time: 20 minutes | Serves 6

1 tablespoon smoked paprika
1 teaspoon coarse salt
1 teaspoon freshly ground black pepper
3 pounds (1.4 kg) turkey breast
1 cup water or chicken stock

1. In a small bowl, mix together the paprika, salt and pepper and rub the mixture all over the outside of the turkey breast.
2. Pour the water or chicken stock into the Instant Pot and insert the steam trivet. Place the turkey breast on the trivet.
3. Secure the lid with the steam vent in the sealed position. Press manual and immediately adjust the timer to 20 minutes. Check that the display light is beneath high pressure.
4. When the timer sounds, quick release the pressure and carefully remove the lid. Remove the turkey breast and place on a carving board. Once cooled enough to handle, thinly slice the turkey and place in an airtight container or resealable plastic bag and store in the refrigerator.

Balsamic Turkey Breast and Red Onions

Prep time: 10 minutes | Cook time: 30 minutes | Serves 4

2½ pounds (1.1 kg) turkey breast, skinless, boneless and sliced
A pinch of salt and black pepper
2 tablespoons balsamic vinegar
1 tablespoon olive oil
1 cup chicken stock
2 cups red onions, sliced
2 tablespoons cilantro, chopped

1. Set your instant pot on Sauté mode, add the oil, heat it up, add the onions and the balsamic vinegar and sauté for 5 minutes.
2. Add the meat and brown for 5 minutes more.
3. Add the rest of the ingredients, put the lid on and cook on High for 20 minutes.
4. Release the pressure naturally for 10 minutes, divide the mix between plates and serve.

Rosemary Turkey Breast

Prep time: 10 minutes | Cook time: 40 minutes | Serves 4 to 6

1 tablespoon extra-virgin olive oil
2 tablespoons ghee or clarified butter
1 (3-pound / 1.4-kg) turkey breast, spine and neck removed
2 tablespoons chopped fresh rosemary
Zest of 1 lemon
2 cloves garlic, grated
Salt and freshly ground black pepper, to taste
1 cup water

1. Pour the olive oil onto the turkey. Rub the ghee all over and even under the skin of the turkey breast.
2. Sprinkle the rosemary, lemon zest, garlic and generous amounts of salt and pepper all over the turkey breast. Use your hands to rub the seasonings all over the turkey and under the skin.
3. Pour the water into the Instant Pot and insert the steam trivet. Place the turkey on top of the trivet, breast/skin side up and bone side down.
4. Secure the lid with the steam vent in the sealed position. Press pressure cook until the display light is beneath high pressure. Use the plus and minus buttons to adjust the time until the display reads "25 minutes."
5. If you are choosing to crisp up the skin, preheat the oven to 450°F (230°C) during this time. Line a large baking sheet with foil.
6. When the timer sounds, quick release the pressure. Remove the lid. Use two sets of tongs to carefully transfer the turkey breast to the prepared baking sheet.
7. Bake the turkey breast in the oven until the skin is nice and golden and crispy, about 15 minutes.
8. Let the turkey rest for 10 minutes before removing the meat from the bones and then slicing.

Thyme Chicken and Brussels Sprouts

Prep time: 5 minutes | Cook time: 25 minutes | Serves 4

2 chicken breasts, skinless, boneless and halved
1 tablespoon olive oil
A pinch of salt and black pepper
2 thyme springs, chopped
2 cups Brussels sprouts, halved
1 cup chicken stock

1. Set your instant pot on sauté mode, add the oil, heat it up, add the meat and brown for 5 minutes.
2. Add the rest of the ingredients, put the lid on and cook on High for 20 minutes.
3. Release the pressure naturally for 10 minutes, divide everything between plates and serve.

Duck Breast with Chives

Prep time: 10 minutes | Cook time: 20 minutes | Serves 4

2 duck breasts, boneless, skin scored and halved
1 tablespoon avocado oil
1 yellow onion, chopped
1 cup chicken stock
A pinch of salt and black pepper
2 teaspoons thyme, dried
1 tablespoon chives, chopped

1. Set the instant pot on Sauté mode, add the oil, heat it up, add the duck breasts skin side down and sear for 2 minutes.
2. Add the rest of the ingredients except the chives, put the lid on and cook on High for 18 minutes.
3. Release the pressure naturally for 10 minutes, divide everything between plates, sprinkle the chives on top and serve.

Fennel Chicken Breast

Prep time: 5 minutes | Cook time: 25 minutes | Serves 4

2 chicken breasts, skinless, boneless and halved
2 tablespoons olive oil
2 tablespoons ginger, grated
2 fennel bulbs, sliced
1 tablespoon basil, chopped
1 cup chicken stock

1. Set your instant pot on sauté mode, add the oil, heat it up, add the ginger and the meat and brown for 5 minutes.
2. Add the rest of the ingredients, put the lid on and cook on High for 20 minutes.
3. Release the pressure naturally for 10 minutes, divide everything between plates and serve.

Savory Chicken Wings

Prep time: 5 minutes | Cook time: 15 minutes | Serves 4

1 cup water or chicken stock
4 pounds (1.8 kg) chicken wings
4 tablespoons ghee or clarified butter, melted
2 tablespoons of your favorite seasoning mix

1. Pour the water or chicken stock into the pot and insert a steamer basket. Place the wings in the steamer basket.
2. Secure the lid with the steam vent in the sealed position. Press manual and immediately adjust the timer to 10 minutes. Check that the display light is beneath high pressure.
3. When the timer sounds, quick release the pressure and carefully remove the lid. Remove the chicken from the pot and place on a broiler pan. Broil until the chicken is browned and crispy, about 5 minutes.
4. In a small bowl, mix together the melted butter and seasoning mix. Brush the wings with the butter mixture and serve immediately.

Mojo Chicken Tacos

Prep time: 10 minutes | Cook time: 15 minutes | Serves 12

¼ cup olive oil
12 chicken breasts, skin and bones removed
8 cloves of garlic, minced
⅔ cup lime juice, freshly squeezed
⅔ cup orange juice, freshly squeezed
1 tablespoon orange peel
1 tablespoon dried oregano
2 tablespoons ground cumin
Salt and pepper
¼ cup cilantro, chopped

1. Press the Sauté button on the Instant Pot.
2. Stir in the chicken breasts and garlic. Cook until the chicken pieces have turned lightly brown.
3. Add the rest of the ingredients except for the cilantro.
4. Close the lid and press the Poultry button.
5. Adjust the cooking time to 15 minutes.
6. Do quick pressure release.
7. Garnish with cilantro.

Butter Chicken Murgh Makhani

Prep time: 10 minutes | Cook time: 20 minutes | Serves 4

1 can crushed tomatoes
6 cloves of garlic
2 teaspoons ginger, grated
1 teaspoon turmeric
½ teaspoon cayenne pepper

1 teaspoon garam masala
1 teaspoon cumin
1-pound (454 g) chicken meat
1 teaspoon paprika

1. Put everything in the Instant Pot.
2. Close the lid and press the Poultry button.
3. Adjust the cooking time to 20 minutes.
4. Do natural pressure release.

Instant Pot Rotisserie Chicken

Prep time: 10 minutes | Cook time: 40 minutes | Serves 6

1 whole chicken
1 ½ teaspoons salt
½ teaspoon pepper
1 teaspoon minced garlic
1 teaspoon paprika
1 ¾ tablespoons olive oil
1 cup chicken broth

1. In a mixing bowl, mix all ingredients except for the chicken broth.
2. Make sure to massage the chicken until all surfaces are covered by the spice rub.
3. Pour the chicken broth into the Instant Pot.
4. Add the chicken.
5. Close the lid and press the Poultry button.
6. Adjust the cooking time to 40 minutes.
7. Do natural pressure release.

Instant Pot Shredded Chicken

Prep time: 5 minutes | Cook time: 30 minutes | Serves 8

4 pounds (1.8 kg) chicken breasts
½ cup water
Salt and pepper to taste

1. Place all ingredients in the Instant Pot.
2. Close the lid and press the Poultry button.
3. Adjust the cooking time to 30 minutes.
4. Do natural pressure release.
5. Use two forks to shred the chicken meat. Remove bones if any.

Moringa Chicken Soup

Prep time: 10 minutes | Cook time: 18 minutes | Serves 8

1½ pounds (680 g) chicken breasts
Salt and pepper
2 cloves of garlic, minced
1 onion, chopped
5 cups water
1 thumb-size ginger
1 cup tomatoes, chopped
2 cups moringa leaves or kale leaves

1. Place all ingredients in the Instant Pot except for the moringa leaves.
2. Close the lid and press the Poultry button.
3. Adjust the cooking time to 15 minutes.
4. Do natural pressure release.
5. Once the lid is open, press the Sauté button.
6. Stir in the moringa leaves and simmer for 3 minutes.

Chicken and Zucchini Noodles

Prep time: 10 minutes | Cook time: 15 minutes | Serves 4

2 chicken breasts, skinless, boneless and halved
3 celery stalks, chopped
1 and ½ cups chicken stock
1 tablespoon tomato sauce
A pinch of salt and black pepper
2 zucchinis, cut with a spiralizer
1 teaspoon chili powder
1 tablespoon cilantro, chopped

1. In your instant pot, mix the chicken with the other ingredients except the zucchini noodles and the cilantro, put the lid on and cook on High for 15 minutes
2. Release the pressure naturally for 10 minutes, set the pot on Sauté mode again, add the zucchini noodles, cook for 5 minutes more, divide between plates and serve with cilantro sprinkled on top.

Chicken and Cucumber Salad

Prep time: 10 minutes | Cook time: 20 minutes | Serves 4

2 chicken breasts, skinless, boneless and halved
1 tablespoon sweet paprika
1 cup chicken stock
1 tablespoon olive oil
1 yellow onion, chopped
½ teaspoon cinnamon powder
2 cucumbers, sliced
1 avocado, peeled, pitted and cubed
1 tomato, cubed
1 tablespoon cilantro, chopped

1. Set instant pot on Sauté mode, add the oil, heat it up, add the onion and the meat and brown for 5 minutes.
2. Add the paprika, stock and the cinnamon, put the lid on and cook on High for 15 minutes.
3. Release the pressure naturally for 10 minutes, and divide the chicken between plates.
4. In a bowl, mix the cucumbers with the avocado, tomato and cilantro, toss, divide the mix next to the chicken and serve.

Garlic Chicken Mix

Prep time: 10 minutes | Cook time: 20 minutes | Serves 4

2 chicken breasts, skinless, boneless and halved
1 cup tomato sauce
1 tablespoon basil, chopped
¼ cup sweet chili sauce
4 garlic cloves, minced
¼ cup chicken stock

1. In your instant pot, combine the chicken with the rest of the ingredients, put the lid on and cook on High for 20 minutes.
2. Release the pressure naturally for 10 minutes, divide everything between plates and serve.

Chicken, Tomato and Bell Peppers

Prep time: 10 minutes | Cook time: 18 minutes | Serves 4

2 chicken breasts, skinless, boneless and cubed
2 tablespoons olive oil
1 teaspoon Creole seasoning
A pinch of cayenne pepper
1 cup tomato, cubed
1 cup mixed bell peppers, cubed
1 yellow onion, chopped
1 cup chicken stock

1. Set the instant pot on Sauté mode, add the oil, heat it up, add the onion and the chicken and brown for 5 minutes.
2. Add the other ingredients, put the lid on and cook on High for 20 minutes.
3. Release the pressure naturally for 10 minutes, divide everything between plates and serve.

Chicken with Mushrooms

Prep time: 15 minutes | Cook time: 30 minutes | serves 4

2 tablespoons extra-virgin olive oil
4 (6-ounce) bone-in, skin-on chicken thighs
1 (4-ounce) package sliced fresh mushrooms
3 celery stalks, chopped
½ of onion, chopped
2 garlic cloves, minced
1 (14-ounce) can stewed tomatoes
2 tablespoons tomato paste
2 teaspoons Herbes de Provence
¾ cup water
Pinch of red pepper flakes
Ground black pepper, as required

1. Add the oil in Instant Pot and select "Sauté". Then add the chicken thighs and cook for about 5-6 minutes per side.
2. With a slotted spoon, transfer chicken thighs onto a plate.
3. In the pot, add the mushrooms, celery and onion and cook for about 5 minutes.
4. Add the garlic and cook for about 2 minutes.
5. Press "Cancel" and stir in the chicken, tomatoes, tomato paste, Herbes de Provence and water.
6. Secure the lid and turn to "Seal" position.
7. Cook on "Manual" with "High Pressure" for about 11 minutes.
8. Press "Cancel" and carefully do a "Quick" release.
9. Remove the lid and stir in red pepper flakes and black pepper.
10. Serve hot.

Sesame Cashew Chicken with Tomato Sauce

Prep time: 15 minutes | Cook time: 15 minutes | Serves 6

2 pounds (907 g) chicken thighs, bones, and skin removed
¼ teaspoon black pepper
¼ cup soy sauce
2 tablespoons rice vinegar
2 tablespoons ketchup
1 tablespoon brown sugar
1 clove of garlic, minced
1 teaspoon grated ginger
1 tablespoon cornstarch + 2 tablespoons water
⅓ cup cashew nuts, toasted
¼ cup green onions, chopped
2 tablespoons sesame seeds, toasted

1. Place all ingredients except for the cornstarch slurry, cashew nuts, green onions, and sesame seeds in the Instant Pot.
2. Give a good stir and close the lid and press the Manual button. Adjust the cooking time to 15 minutes.
3. Do quick pressure release. Once the lid is open, press the Sauté button and stir in the slurry. Allow simmering until the sauce thickens.
4. Stir in the cashew nuts, green onions, and sesame seeds last.

Thyme-Stewed 40-Clove Chicken

Prep time: 10 minutes | Cook time: 20 minutes | Serves 6

1 tablespoon olive oil
1 tablespoon butter
4 chicken thighs, bone and skin not removed
2 chicken breasts, bone and skin not removed
Salt and pepper
40 cloves of garlic, peeled and sliced
2 sprigs of thyme
¼ cup dry white wine
¼ cup chicken broth
Parsley for garnish

1. Press the Sauté button on the Instant Pot.
2. Pour the oil and butter. Stir in the chicken pieces and season with salt and pepper to taste.
3. Add the garlic cloves. Continue stirring for 5 minutes until fragrant. Stir in the thyme, white wine, and chicken broth.
4. Place all ingredients except for the cornstarch slurry, sesame seeds, and green onions in the Instant Pot. Give a good stir.
5. Close the lid and press the Manual button. Adjust the cooking time to 15 minutes.
6. Do quick pressure release. Once the lid is open, garnish with parsley.

Orange Marmalade Chicken Stew

Prep time: 10 minutes | Cook time: 15 minutes | Serves 4

4 chicken breasts
¾ cup barbecue sauce
2 tablespoons soy sauce
¾ cup orange marmalade
¼ cup water
1 tablespoon cornstarch + 2 tablespoons water
2 tablespoons green onions, chopped

1. Place all ingredients except for the cornstarch slurry and green onions in the Instant Pot.
2. Give a good stir. Close the lid and press the Poultry button. Adjust the cooking time to 15 minutes.
3. Do quick pressure release. Once the lid is open, press the Sauté button and stir in the cornstarch slurry.
4. Simmer until the sauce thickens. Stir in green onions last.

Chinese Sweet and Sour Chicken

Prep time: 10 minutes | Cook time: 15 minutes | Serves 8

2 pounds (907 g) chicken meat
4 cloves of garlic, minced
1 onion, chopped
1 green bell pepper, julienned
½ cup ketchup
½ cup molasses
¼ cup soy sauce
1 tablespoon cornstarch + 2 tablespoons water

1. Press the Sauté button on the Instant Pot.
2. Place the chicken, garlic, and onion. Stir to combine everything and until the chicken meat has turned lightly golden. Stir in the bell pepper, ketchup, molasses, and soy sauce.
3. Close the lid and press the Poultry button. Adjust the cooking time to 15 minutes.
4. Do quick pressure release. Once the lid is open, press the Sauté button and stir in the cornstarch slurry. Allow simmering until the sauce thickens.

Balsamic Peppery Chicken with Chopped Tomato

Prep time: 10 minutes | Cook time: 20 minutes | Serves 4

1 can crushed tomatoes
6 cloves of garlic
2 teaspoons ginger, grated
1 teaspoon turmeric
½ teaspoon cayenne pepper
1 teaspoon paprika
1 teaspoon garam masala
1 teaspoon cumin
1-pound (454 g) chicken meat

1. Put everything in the Instant Pot.
2. Close the lid and press the Poultry button.
3. Adjust the cooking time to 20 minutes.
4. Do natural pressure release.

Garlicky Rotisserie Chicken

Prep time: 10 minutes | Cook time: 40 minutes | Serves 6

1 whole chicken
1 ½ teaspoons salt
½ teaspoon pepper
1 teaspoon minced garlic
1 teaspoon paprika
1 ¾ tablespoons olive oil
1 cup chicken broth

1. In a mixing bowl, mix all ingredients except for the chicken broth.
2. Make sure to massage the chicken until all surfaces are covered by the spice rub.
3. Pour the chicken broth into the Instant Pot.
4. Add the chicken.
5. Close the lid and press the Poultry button.
6. Adjust the cooking time to 40 minutes.
7. Do natural pressure release.

Salty Shredded Chicken

Prep time: 5 minutes | Cook time: 30 minutes | Serves 8

4 pounds (1.8 kg) chicken breasts
½ cup water
Salt and pepper, to taste

1. Place all ingredients in the Instant Pot.
2. Close the lid and press the Poultry button.
3. Adjust the cooking time to 30 minutes.
4. Do natural pressure release.
5. Use two forks to shred the chicken meat. Remove bones if any.

Chicken Mix Avocado and Cucumbers

Prep time: 10 minutes | Cook time: 20 minutes | Serves 4

2 chicken breasts, skinless, boneless
   and halved
1 tablespoon sweet paprika
1 cup chicken stock
1 tablespoon olive oil
1 yellow onion, chopped
½ teaspoon cinnamon powder
2 cucumbers, sliced
1 avocado, peeled, pitted and cubed
1 tomato, cubed
1 tablespoon cilantro, chopped

1. Set instant pot on Sauté mode, add the oil, heat it up, add the onion and the meat and brown for 5 minutes.
2. Add the paprika, stock and the cinnamon, put the lid on and cook on High for 15 minutes.
3. Release the pressure naturally for 10 minutes, and divide the chicken between plates.
4. In a bowl, mix the cucumbers with the avocado, tomato and cilantro, toss, divide the mix next to the chicken and serve.

Chicken Mix Peppers and Tomato

Prep time: 10 minutes | Cook time: 18 minutes | Serves 4

2 chicken breasts, skinless, boneless
   and cubed
2 tablespoons olive oil
1 teaspoon Creole seasoning
A pinch of cayenne pepper
1 cup tomato, cubed
1 cup mixed bell peppers, cubed
1 yellow onion, chopped
1 cup chicken stock

1. Set the instant pot on Sauté mode, add the oil, heat it up, add the onion and the chicken and brown for 5 minutes.
2. Add the other ingredients, put the lid on and cook on High for 20 minutes.
3. Release the pressure naturally for 10 minutes, divide everything between plates and serve.

Chapter 7 Beef and Lamb

Sloppy Joe–Stuffed Mushrooms

Prep time: 15 minutes | Cook time: 13 minutes | Serves 4

4 (3- to 4-ounce / 85- to 113-g) medium portobello mushrooms

3 green onions

1 pound (454 g) ground beef

1 small red bell pepper, chopped

1 small stalk celery, thinly sliced

½ cup Whole30-compliant beef broth

⅓ cup Whole30-compliant tomato paste

2 to 3 tablespoons balsamic vinegar

2 cloves garlic, minced

1 teaspoon dried oregano

½ teaspoon salt

½ teaspoon black pepper

¼ cup chopped fresh parsley

1. Use a damp cloth or paper towel to wipe the mushrooms. Remove the stems from the mushrooms and chop; set aside. Using a small spoon, scrape the gills from the mushroom caps and discard. Set the mushrooms aside. Thinly slice the green onions; separate the white and green parts.
2. On a 6-quart Instant Pot, select Sauté and adjust to Normal/Medium. Add the chopped mushroom stems, white parts of the green onions, the ground beef, bell pepper, and celery. Cook, stirring with a wooden spoon to break up the meat, until the meat is browned, about 10 minutes. Press Cancel. Drain any fat.
3. Add the broth, tomato paste, 2 tablespoons of the vinegar, the garlic, oregano, salt, and pepper to the meat mixture. Stir until well combined. Place the mushroom caps, stemmed sides down, over the meat mixture, overlapping them slightly, if needed. Lock the lid in place.
4. Select Manual and cook on high pressure for 3 minutes. Use natural release.
5. Transfer the mushrooms to serving plates, stemmed sides up. Stir the meat mixture. If desired, stir in the remaining 1 tablespoon vinegar. Spoon the meat mixture on the mushrooms. Sprinkle with the reserved green onion green parts and the parsley.

Beef and Lamb Mix with Veggie

Prep time: 10 minutes | Cook time: 20 minutes | Serves 4

1 pound (454 g) beef stew meat, cubed

1 pound (454 g) lamb shoulder, cubed

4 garlic cloves, minced

2 red bell peppers, cut into strips

1 tablespoon olive oil

2 celery stalks, chopped

2 carrots, chopped

¼ teaspoon thyme, dried

A pinch of salt and black pepper

1 tablespoon oregano, chopped

1½ cups beef stock

1. Set your instant pot on Sauté mode, add the oil, heat it up, add the garlic and the meat and brown for 5 minutes.
2. Add the rest of the ingredients, put the lid on and cook on High for 30 minutes.
3. Release the pressure fast for 5 minutes, divide the mix between plates and serve.

Spicy Minced Lamb Meat

Prep time: 10 minutes | Cook time: 20 minutes | Serves 2

½ pound (227 g) ground lamb meat
½ cup onion; chopped
¼ teaspoon cumin
¼ teaspoon cayenne pepper
½ tablespoons garlic
½ tablespoons minced ginger
¼ teaspoon turmeric
¼ teaspoon ground coriander
½ teaspoon salt

1. Set the instant pot to Sauté mode,
2. Add the onions; garlic and ginger and sauté for 5 minutes,
3. Add the remaining Ingredients to the pot and secure the lid.
4. Cook on the Manual function for 15 minutes at high pressure,
5. When it beeps; Natural Release the steam for 15 minutes, Remove the lid and serve immediately.

Texas Brisket Chili with Veggie

Prep time: 25 minutes | Cook time: 1¼ hours | Serves 6

3 pounds (1.4 kg) flat cut brisket, excess fat trimmed and cut into 1-inch cubes
1½ teaspoons kosher salt
1 teaspoon freshly ground black pepper
2 tablespoons extra virgin olive oil
1 medium yellow onion, diced
1 medium green bell pepper, seeded and diced
4 garlic cloves, minced
2 tablespoons tomato paste
1 teaspoon chili powder
1 teaspoon ground cumin
2 dried bay leaves
1 teaspoon dried oregano
½ teaspoon chipotle chili powder
½ teaspoon smoked paprika
1 (14½-ounce / 411.1-g) can diced fire-roasted tomatoes
½ cup low-sodium beef broth or water
¼ cup mild roasted green chiles (from a jar)
1 tablespoon balsamic vinegar
1 (15-ounce / 425-g) can pinto beans, drained and rinsed (omit for Whole30, paleo)

For Serving: (optional)
2 green onions (green parts only), sliced (½ cup)
2 radishes, cut into matchsticks

1. Season the cubed brisket with the salt and pepper.
2. Heat the olive oil in an Instant Pot on the sauté function until it shimmers. Working in batches, brown the meat on all sides, about 90 seconds per side. Transfer to a bowl and set aside.
3. Add the onion, bell pepper, and garlic to the pot and use the sauté function to cook, stirring occasionally, until slightly tender, about 4 minutes. Add the tomato paste, chili powder, cumin, bay leaves, oregano, chipotle chili powder, and paprika and cook while stirring for 1 minute.
4. Return the browned brisket and all of its juices to the pot along with the fire-roasted tomatoes, broth or water, green chiles, and balsamic vinegar. Stir until well combined, then turn off the heat by hitting the cancel button.
5. Secure the lid onto the Instant Pot and be sure the vent is sealed. Hit the meat/stew button and set the cook time to 60 minutes on high pressure. When done, carefully release the pressure by turning the valve on top of the Instant Pot. Once the steam has fully released, carefully remove the lid.
6. Add the drained and rinsed pinto beans (if using) and stir to combine; keep the Instant Pot on warm until heated through, about 5 more minutes. Remove and discard the bay leaves. Serve the chili on its own or topped with green onions, radishes.

Beef Pot Roast

Prep time: 5 minutes | Cook time: 1 hour | Serves 8

1 tablespoon olive oil
1 onion, chopped
3 cloves of garlic
3 pounds (1.4 kg) beef pot roast
1 bag frozen vegetables of your choice
1 cup beef broth
Salt and pepper, to taste

1. Press the Sauté button on the Instant Pot.
2. Heat the oil and sauté the onions and garlic.
3. Stir in the beef pot roast and sear all sides until lightly golden.
4. Stir in the rest of the ingredients.
5. Close the lid and press the Meat/Stew button.
6. Adjust the cooking time to 60 minutes.
7. Do natural pressure release.

Instant Pot Korean Beef

Prep time: 15 minutes | Cook time: 15 minutes | Serves 12

6 pounds (2.7 kg) beef chuck roast cubed
1 teaspoon sea salt
1 cup bone broth or beef broth
1 cup coconut aminos
0.5 apple diced
4 tablespoon rice vinegar or apple cider vinegar
2 tablespoon sesame oil
8 garlic cloves
2 inch ginger
2 teaspoon onion powder
Optional: 2 teaspoon Gochugaru or more, for spice
1 teaspoon ground black pepper
4 tablespoon arrowroot starch
4 tablespoon water
Sesame seeds and chopped green onions for garnish

1. Add cubed chuck roast to the Instant pot liner and toss with sea salt to coat evenly.
2. In a blender, add bone broth, coconut aminos, apple, rice vinegar, sesame oil, garlic, ginger, onion powder, Gochugaru (if using), and ground black pepper. Blend until smooth and creamy.
3. Pour the sauce over the meat and stir. Set the instant pot to manual for 15 minutes.
4. Once the Instant Pot beeps to a finish, open the pressure valve immediately to release pressure.
5. Open the lid, and the set the instant pot to SAUTÉ.
6. Stir together arrowroot starch and water in a separate bowl, then pour into the instant pot. Simmer for a few minutes so the sauce thickens. Turn off heat.
7. Serve sprinkled with chopped green onions and sesame seeds.

Beef Cube and Sun-Dried Tomatoes

Prep time: 10 minutes | Cook time: 25 minutes | Serves 4

1½ pounds (680 g) beef stew meat, cubed
1 yellow onion, chopped
1½ cups sun-dried tomatoes, chopped
3 garlic cloves, minced
1 cup beef stock
1 teaspoon sweet paprika
1 tablespoon olive oil
A pinch of salt and black pepper

1. Set your instant pot on Sauté mode, add the oil, heat it up, add the onion and garlic and cook for 2 minutes.
2. Add the meat and brown for 3 minutes.
3. Add the rest of the ingredients, put the lid on and cook on High for 20 minutes.
4. Release the pressure naturally for 10 minutes, divide the mix between plates and serve.

Rich and Saucy Beef Lettuce Wraps

Prep time: 15 minutes | Cook time: 20 minutes | Serves 4

1 tablespoon clarified butter or ghee
1 pound (454 g) lean ground beef
½ teaspoon salt
½ teaspoon black pepper
1 large onion, diced
1 medium red bell pepper, diced
2 cloves garlic, minced
1 jalapeño, diced
1 teaspoon smoked paprika
1 teaspoon chili powder
½ teaspoon Korean pepper flakes (optional)
½ teaspoon ground coriander
¼ teaspoon ground cumin
1 tablespoon coconut aminos
1 cup Whole30-compliant canned crushed tomatoes
12 Boston or Bibb lettuce leaves
1 avocado, halved, pitted, peeled, and sliced
Chopped fresh cilantro, for garnish

1. On a 6-quart Instant Pot, select Sauté and adjust to More/High. Add the butter to the pot. When it's hot, add the beef and cook, stirring to break up with a wooden spoon, until browned, about 5 minutes. Season with the salt and pepper. Add the onion, bell pepper, garlic, and jalapeño. Cook, stirring occasionally, until the vegetables are tender, about 5 minutes. Stir in the paprika, chili powder, Korean pepper flakes, coriander, and cumin. Add the coconut aminos and crushed tomatoes. Stir, scraping the browned bits on the bottom of the pot. Lock the lid in place.
2. Select Meat/Stew and cook for 10 minutes. Use natural release for 10 minutes, then use quick release.
3. Serve the meat mixture in the lettuce leaves. Top with avocado slices and cilantro.

Picadillo Beef Chuck Roast with Veggie

Prep time: 15 minutes | Cook time: 1¼ hours | Serves 6

2 tablespoons extra-virgin olive oil

1 medium yellow onion, finely chopped

1 medium red bell pepper, finely chopped

4 cloves garlic, minced

1 (2- to 2½-pound / 907- to 1135-g) boneless beef chuck roast, cut into 3 or 4 pieces

1 (8-ounce / 227-g) can Whole30-compliant tomato sauce

1 tablespoon red wine vinegar

2 teaspoons ground cumin

2 teaspoons dried oregano

1 teaspoon salt

¼ teaspoon black pepper

6 medium Yukon Gold potatoes, quartered

½ cup quartered pitted Whole30-compliant manzanilla olives or other green olives

⅓ cup unsulfured golden raisins

¼ cup Whole30-compliant capers, drained

1. On a 6-quart Instant Pot, select Sauté and adjust to Normal/Medium. Add the olive oil. When it's hot, add the onion, bell pepper, and garlic and cook, stirring occasionally, until softened, 3 to 5 minutes. Add the beef and cook until browned, about 5 minutes. Press Cancel. Add the tomato sauce, vinegar, cumin, oregano, salt, and pepper; stir to combine. Lock the lid in place.
2. Select Manual and cook on high pressure for 50 minutes. Use quick release.
3. Add the potatoes, olives, raisins, and capers. Lock the lid in place. Select Manual and cook on high pressure for 8 minutes. Use quick release.
4. Use a slotted spoon to remove the potatoes, vegetables, and beef. Use two forks to shred the beef. Serve the beef and vegetables over the potatoes.

Lamb Steak Tagine

Prep time: 10 minutes | Cook time: 38 minutes | Serves 4

2½ pounds (1.1 kg) blade lamb steaks, meat cut off the bones into 1½-inch chunks, bones reserved

2 tablespoons olive oil

Salt and freshly ground black pepper, to taste

1 medium yellow onion, sliced through root end

4 teaspoons ras el hanout seasoning

1½ cups beef broth

2 large carrots, peeled and cut into 1-inch pieces

¼ cup dates, pitted and roughly chopped

¼ cup oil-packed sun-dried tomatoes, chopped

1 tablespoon white wine vinegar

Optional garnishes

Cooked couscous

Harissa

1. Select SAUTÉ and adjust to MORE/HIGH heat. Toss the lamb meat with the oil and season all over with salt and several grinds of pepper. When the pot is hot, add half the meat and cook, stirring occasionally, until browned, 8 minutes.
2. Add the remaining lamb, the onion, and ras el hanout to the pot and cook, stirring occasionally, until the onion softens, 5 minutes. Add the broth, carrots, dates, and sun-dried tomatoes. Place the bones in the pot on top of the other ingredients. Press CANCEL.
3. Lock on the lid, select PRESSURE COOK, and adjust to HIGH pressure for 25 minutes. Make sure the steam valve is in the "Sealing" position. (Or you can SLOW COOK it—see instructions below.) When the cooking time is up, let the pressure come down naturally for 15 minutes and then quick-release any remaining pressure. Discard the bones.
4. Select SAUTÉ and adjust to MORE/HIGH heat. Add the vinegar to the pot and stir to combine. When the liquid comes to a simmer, use a ladle to spoon off most of the liquid fat that pools around the edges of the pot. Press CANCEL. Season with salt and pepper. If desired, serve over couscous with dabs of harissa.

Beef Chuck Roast Chili

Prep time: 10 minutes | Cook time: 1 hour | Serves 6

1 tablespoon oil

2 pounds (907 g) beef chuck roast, cut into cubes

Salt and pepper, to taste

1 tablespoon chili powder

2 tablespoons cumin powder

1 tablespoon paprika

1 cup beef broth

8 ounces (227 g) portobello mushrooms, chopped

1 tablespoon onion powder

1 can tomato paste

1 can crushed tomatoes

1. Press the Sauté button on the Instant Pot.
2. Heat the oil and sauté the beef chuck roast until lightly golden on all sides.
3. Season with salt and pepper to taste.
4. Stir in the rest of the ingredients.
5. Close the lid and press the Meat/Stew button.
6. Adjust the cooking time to 60 minutes.
7. Do natural pressure release.

Italian Chuck Sauce

Prep time: 10 minutes | Cook time: 19 minutes | Serves 6

1 tablespoon olive oil
1 pound (454 g) 95% lean ground chuck
1 medium yellow onion, chopped
3 tablespoons tomato paste
3 medium garlic cloves, chopped
2 teaspoons Italian seasoning
1 (28-ounce / 794-g) can San Marzano–
    style tomatoes, chopped, with juice
½ cup beef broth
Salt and freshly ground black pepper, to
    taste

1. Put the oil in the pot, select SAUTÉ, and adjust to MORE/HIGH heat. When the oil is hot, add the ground beef and onion and cook, stirring frequently, until the meat is cooked and the onion is tender, 8 minutes. Leave some of the beef in large chunks for the best texture.
2. Push the meat and onion mixture to one side of the pot. Add the tomato paste, garlic, and Italian seasoning to the other side of the pot and cook until fragrant, 1 minute. Press CANCEL.
3. Add the tomatoes and the broth to the pot. Lock on the lid, select the PRESSURE COOK function, and adjust to HIGH pressure for 10 minutes. Make sure the steam valve is in the "Sealing" position.
4. When the cooking time is up, quick-release the pressure. Season the sauce with salt and pepper and serve.

Basic Beef Short Ribs

Prep time: 5 minutes | Cook time: 40 minutes | Serves 12

1 tablespoon oil
1 onion, chopped
3 cloves of garlic, minced
4 pounds (1.8 kg) beef short ribs
Salt and pepper, to taste
1 cup water

1. Press the Sauté button on the Instant Pot.
2. Heat the olive oil and sauté the onions.
3. Add in the short ribs and the rest of the ingredients.
4. Close the lid and press the Meat/Stew button.
5. Adjust the cooking time to 40 minutes.
6. Do natural pressure release.

Beef and Bacon Chili

Prep time: 10 minutes | Cook time: 38 minutes | Serves 4

1 pound (454 g) Whole30-compliant bacon,
    chopped
1 pound (454 g) lean ground beef
2 tablespoons mild chili powder
½ teaspoon salt
1 (28-ounce / 794-g) can Whole30-compliant
    diced tomatoes, undrained
1 cup Whole30-compliant beef broth
1 medium onion, chopped
1 medium red bell pepper, chopped
1 medium jalapeño, seeded and chopped
2 cloves garlic, minced
Chopped fresh cilantro (optional)

1. On a 6-quart Instant Pot, select Sauté and adjust to Normal/Medium. Add the bacon and cook, stirring occasionally, until crisp, about 10 minutes. Transfer the bacon to paper towels.
2. Add the ground beef to the bacon drippings in the pot. Cook, stirring frequently, until browned, 8 to 10 minutes. Drain off the fat, if needed. Return three-fourths of the bacon to the pot. Stir in the chili powder and salt. Stir in the tomatoes, broth, onion, bell pepper, jalapeño, and garlic. Lock the lid in place.
3. Select Manual and cook on high pressure for 20 minutes. Use quick release.
4. Serve the chili topped with the remaining bacon, and cilantro if desired.

Peppery BBQ Beef Ribs

Prep time: 5 minutes | Cook time: 1 hour | Serves 7

3 pounds (1.4 kg) beef ribs
Salt and pepper, to taste
2 cups Whole30-compliant BBQ sauce
2 tablespoons pepper jelly
½ cup beef broth

1. Season the ribs with salt and pepper.
2. Place in the Instant Pot and pour over the rest of the ingredients.
3. Close the lid and press the Meat/Stew button.
4. Adjust the cooking time to 60 minutes.
5. Do natural pressure release.

Beef Chili with Pumpkin and Root Vegetable

Prep time: 15 minutes | Cook time: 8 minutes | Serves 4 to 6

1 tablespoon olive oil
1 pound (454 g) beef, cut into chunks
1 cup pumpkin, peeled and cubed
2 carrots, peeled and diced
14 ounces (397 g) can tomatoes, diced
2 cups sweet potatoes, peeled and diced
½ large onion, diced
8 ounces (227 g) can tomato sauce
3 cloves garlic
1 teaspoon garlic powder
½ teaspoon salt
½ teaspoon pepper or to taste
2 teaspoons taco seasoning

1. Select the SAUTÉ setting on the Instant Pot and heat the oil.
2. Brown the beef chunks for 4 minutes on both sides.
3. Add the pumpkin, carrots, tomatoes, sweet potatoes, onion, tomato sauce, cloves garlic, garlic powder, salt, pepper and taco seasoning. Stir well.
4. Press the CANCEL key to stop the SAUTÉ function.
5. Close and lock the lid. Select the MEAT/STEW setting and leave it on the default.
6. Once cooking is complete, select CANCEL and let Naturally Release for 10 minutes. Release any remaining steam manually. Uncover the pot.
7. Slightly mash the sweet potatoes with a fork, stir and let the dish sit for 15 minutes.
8. Serve.

Beef, Mushroom, and Sweet Potato Pot

Prep time: 15 minutes | Cook time: 20 minutes | Serves 4

2 tablespoons olive oil
1 pound (454 g) ground beef
1 small onion, finely chopped
1 carrot, peeled and chopped
1 celery stick, chopped
¾ cup chopped baby Bella mushrooms
1 garlic clove, minced
2 tablespoons tomato paste
1 tablespoon Worcestershire Sauce
1 teaspoon cinnamon powder
2 cups beef stock
2 sweet potatoes, chopped

1. Set to Sauté, heat olive oil and brown beef for 5 minutes. Mix in onion, carrot, celery, mushrooms, and garlic. Cook until veggies soften, 5 minutes. Mix in tomato paste, Worcestershire sauce, and cinnamon. Cook further for 1 minute.
2. Pour in beef stock and potatoes; stir. Seal the lid, select Pressure Cook on High, and set to 10 minutes. After cooking, allow a natural release and unlock the lid. Stir and adjust taste with salt and pepper. Dish food and serve warm.

Round Roast and Mushroom and Potato

Prep time: 10 minutes | Cook time: 35 minutes | Serves 6

2½ pounds (1.1 kg) round roast (top or bottom)
2 tablespoons olive oil
2 cups vegetable or beef broth
2 tablespoons minced garlic
1 teaspoon kosher salt
½ teaspoon ground black pepper
1 tablespoon thyme
2 to 3 cups sliced mushrooms
1 large white onion, sliced or diced
1 pound (454 g) potatoes, quartered or cubed

1. Add the olive oil, broth, garlic, salt, pepper, and thyme to the pot, Mix well.
2. Add the roast, mushrooms, and onion, stir.
3. Close and lock the lid. Select MANUAL and cook at HIGH pressure for 25 minutes.
4. When the timer goes off, use a quick release. Carefully open the lid.
5. Add the potatoes, stir.
6. Close and lock the lid. Select MANUAL and cook at HIGH pressure for another 10 minutes.
7. When the timer beeps, use a Quick Release. Carefully unlock the lid.
8. Serve.

Beef Short Ribs and Carrot

Prep time: 10 minutes | Cook time: 46 minutes | Serves 6 to 8

4 pounds (1.8 kg) beef short ribs
1 teaspoon kosher salt
1 teaspoon ground black pepper
2 tablespoons olive oil
3 cloves garlic, minced
4 to 6 carrots, cut into bite sized pieces
2 cups onions, diced
1 tablespoon dried thyme
1½ cups beef broth

1. Rinse and pat the ribs dry with paper towels.
2. Season the ribs with salt and pepper
3. Set your instant pot on SAUTÉ mode, add the oil and heat it up.
4. Add the ribs to the pot and cook for 5 minutes on each side, until browned. Brown the short ribs in batches.
5. Transfer the browned ribs to a plate.
6. Add the garlic to the pot and cook for 1 minute.
7. Put the carrot, onion and thyme to the pot. Sauté for another 5 minutes, until softened.
8. Add the broth and deglaze the pot by scraping the bottom to remove all of the brown bits.
9. Put the beef ribs back into the pot.
10. Press the CANCEL button to reset the cooking program, then select the MANUAL setting and set the cooking time for 35 minutes at HIGH pressure.
11. Once cooking is complete, select CANCEL and let Naturally Release for 15 minutes. Release any remaining steam manually. Uncover the pot.
12. Serve with potato or veggies.

Coffee-Braised Beef with Guacamole

Prep time: 15 minutes | Cook time: 1¼ hours | Serves 4

2 teaspoons cumin seeds
1 teaspoon garlic powder
1½ teaspoons salt
1 teaspoon black pepper
1 (2- to 2½-pound / 0.9- to 1.1-kg) boneless beef chuck pot roast, trimmed
1 tablespoon olive oil
1 cup brewed coffee
1 medium yellow onion, cut into thin wedges
2 avocados, halved, peeled, seeded, and coarsely chopped
Grated zest and juice of ½ lime
1 jalapeño, seeded and minced
1 head iceberg or butter lettuce
4 medium radishes, sliced
¼ cup chopped fresh cilantro

1. In a small bowl, combine the cumin seeds, garlic powder, 1 teaspoon of the salt, and the pepper. Rub the spice mixture over the roast. Select Sauté on a 6-quart Instant Pot. Add the olive oil. When the oil is hot, add the roast. Cook until browned on all sides, about 10 minutes. Press Cancel. Add the coffee and onion to the pot. Lock the lid in place.
2. Select Manual and cook on high pressure for 60 minutes. Use natural release.
3. Meanwhile, for the guacamole, in a medium bowl combine the avocado, lime zest and juice, and jalapeño. Season with the remaining ½ teaspoon salt.
4. Use a slotted spoon to transfer the beef and onions to a large bowl or platter. Discard the cooking liquid. Use two forks to shred the beef. Serve the beef and onion in lettuce leaves with the guacamole, radishes, and cilantro.

Corned Beef and Vegetable

Prep time: 5 minutes | Cook time: 1½ hours | Serves 4

1 cup beef stock
3 pounds (1.4 kg) corned beef
1 pound (454 g) baby potatoes, quartered
1 pound (454 g) baby carrots
1 head cabbage, thickly sliced, core removed

1. In the Instant Pot, combine the beef stock and the corned beef along with the contents of its seasoning packet.
2. Secure the lid with the steam vent in the sealed position. Press manual and immediately adjust the timer to 80 minutes. Check that the display light is beneath high pressure.
3. When the timer sounds, quick release the pressure and carefully remove the lid. Remove the corned beef and place on a serving platter. Tent with foil to keep warm and prevent the beef from drying out.
4. Add the potatoes, carrots and cabbage to the pot. Secure the lid with the steam vent in the sealed position. Press manual and immediately adjust the timer to 4 minutes. Check that the display light is beneath high pressure.
5. When the timer sounds, quick release the pressure and carefully remove the lid. Transfer the potatoes, carrots and cabbage to the serving platter, then drizzle some of the juice from the pot over everything. Serve immediately.

Fresh Herb Beef Rump Roast

Prep time: 10 minutes | Cook time: 1 hour | Serves 6 to 8

8 tablespoons ghee or clarified butter, divided

2 to 3 pounds (0.9- to 1.4-kg) grass-fed beef rump roast

1 large yellow onion, thickly sliced

3 large celery ribs, thinly sliced

5 cloves garlic, chopped

1 teaspoon chopped fresh thyme leaves

1 teaspoon chopped fresh rosemary leaves

¾ cup filtered water, or beef or chicken stock

¼ cup coconut aminos

¼ cup finely chopped fresh parsley

1 teaspoon sea salt

1. Place 2 tablespoons of the butter in the Instant Pot and press sauté. Once the butter has melted, add the roast and brown for about 3½ minutes per side. Remove the roast and transfer to a plate. Set aside. Add the remaining 6 tablespoons of butter and the onion, celery, garlic, thyme and rosemary to the pot and sauté, stirring occasionally, for 5 minutes, or until fragrant. Add the filtered water or stock and coconut aminos, giving the mixture a quick stir and scraping up any browned bits with a wooden spoon. Add the parsley and salt, then give the mixture another stir. Press keep warm/cancel.
2. Place the browned roast in the Instant Pot. Secure the lid with the steam vent in the sealed position. Press manual and set on high pressure for 40 minutes.
3. Once the timer sounds, press keep warm/cancel. Allow the Instant Pot to release pressure naturally for 15 minutes. Using an oven mitt, do a quick release. If there is any steam left over, allow it to release until the silver dial drops, then carefully open the lid.
4. Carefully remove the roast, place on a large plate or cutting board and cut into shredded chunks. Add the shredded beef back to the Instant Pot. Secure the lid with the steam vent in the sealed position. Press manual and set on high pressure for 5 minutes.
5. Once the timer sounds, press keep warm/cancel. Using an oven mitt, do a quick release. When the steam venting stops and the silver dial drops, carefully open the lid.
6. To reduce the sauce, press sauté and allow the sauce and shredded beef to simmer for 5 to 10 minutes to thicken. Once the sauce has reduced, allow the shredded beef to rest in the Instant Pot for about 15 minutes before serving.
7. Serve immediately or refrigerate for later use.

Beef Brisket and Vegetable

Prep time: 10 minutes | Cook time: 1 hour | Serves 4 to 6

2½ pounds (1.1 kg) beef brisket

1 teaspoon salt

½ teaspoon ground black pepper

3 cloves garlic, chopped

2 bay leaves

4 cups water

1 cabbage heat, cut into 6 wedges

4 carrots, chopped

3 turnips, cut into quarters

6 potatoes, cut into quarters

Horseradish sauce for serving

1. Add the beef brisket to the Instant Pot and season with salt and pepper.
2. Add the garlic and bay leaves. Pour the water into the pot.
3. Close and lock the lid. Select the MANUAL setting and set the cooking time for 60 minutes at HIGH pressure.
4. Once cooking is complete, use a Quick Release the pressure. Open the lid.
5. Add the cabbage, carrots, turnips, and potatoes to the pot.
6. Close and lock the lid. Select MANUAL and cook at HIGH pressure for 6 minutes.
7. Once cooking is complete, select Cancel and use a Natural Release for 10 minutes. Uncover the pot.
8. Serve with horseradish sauce.

Swiss Beef Round Steak

Prep time: 5 minutes | Cook time: 20 minutes | Serves 6

1½ pounds (680 g) beef round steak, cut into 6 pieces

½ teaspoon salt

¼ teaspoon pepper

1 medium onion, cut into ¼-in. slices

1 celery rib, cut into ½-in. slices

2 (8-ounce / 227-g) cans tomato sauce

1. Sprinkle the steak with salt and pepper. Place the onion in a 6-qt. electric pressure cooker. Top with the celery, tomato sauce and steak. Lock lid; close pressure-release valve. Adjust to pressure-cook on high for 20 minutes. Let pressure release naturally for 5 minutes; quick-release any remaining pressure. A thermometer inserted in steak should read at least 145°F (63°C).

Shredded Pepper Steak

Prep time: 5 minutes | Cook time: 1 ¼ hours | Serves 6 to 8

3 to 4 pounds (1.4- to 1.8-kg) beef (cheap steak or roast cuts will all work)
1 tablespoon garlic powder
Red chili flakes, to taste
1 (16-ounce / 454-g) jar mild pepper rings (banana peppers or pepperoncini)
½ cup salted beef broth

1. Add beef to the Instant Pot and season with garlic powder and red chili.
2. Pour the pepper rings and broth into the pot, stir.
3. Close and lock the lid. Select the MANUAL setting and set the cooking time for 70 minutes at HIGH pressure.
4. Once cooking is complete, use a Natural Release for 10 minutes, then release any remaining pressure manually. Open the lid.
5. Shred the meat in the pot (or transfer to a plate) and stir. Serve.

Balsamic Beef Short Ribs

Prep time: 10 minutes | Cook time: 1 hour | Serves 4 to 6

2 teaspoons olive oil
2 pounds (907 g) boneless beef short ribs
1 medium onion, chopped
1 medium carrot, diced
3 cloves garlic, minced
4 sprigs thyme
2 tablespoons balsamic vinegar
2 tablespoons ghee or clarified butter
Coarse salt, to taste
Freshly ground black pepper, to taste

1. Press sauté to preheat the Instant Pot. When the word "hot" appears on the display, add the olive oil. When the oil is shimmering, add the short ribs and brown on all sides, about 10 minutes. Remove the ribs and set them aside.
2. Add the onion and carrot to the pot. Cook until the onion is starting to soften, about 5 minutes. Add the garlic and sauté for about another minute, stirring frequently. Add the thyme sprigs and vinegar, stirring well to scrape up any browned bits from the bottom. Cook until the liquid is reduced by half, about 5 minutes. Press cancel to turn off the Instant Pot.
3. Return the ribs to the pot. Secure the lid with the steam vent in the sealed position. Press manual and immediately adjust the timer to 40 minutes. Check that the display light is beneath high pressure.
4. When the timer sounds, quick release the pressure and carefully remove the lid. Remove the ribs and place on a serving platter.
5. Stir the ghee or clarified butter into the liquid left in the pot and season to taste with salt and pepper. Pour the sauce over the ribs and serve.

Beef Chuck Roast

Prep time: 5 minutes | Cook time: 1 ½ hours | Serves 4 to 6

3½ pounds (1.6 kg) beef chuck roast
2 tablespoons olive oil
1 teaspoon sea salt
2½ cups beef broth

1. Preheat the Instant Pot by selecting SAUTÉ. Add the oil.
2. Season the meat with salt.
3. Add the beef roast to the pot and sauté for 8 to 10 minutes on both sides, until browned.
4. Close and lock the lid. Press the CANCEL button to reset the cooking program, then select the MANUAL setting and set the cooking time for 75 minutes at HIGH pressure.
5. Once cooking is complete, select CANCEL and let Naturally Release for 10 minutes. Release any remaining steam manually. Uncover the pot.
6. Remove the beef roast from the pot and shred the meat with 2 forks.
7. Return to the Instant Pot and stir with remaining liquid.
8. Serve with potato.

Chunky and Beanless Beef Chili

Prep time: 15 minutes | Cook time: 60 minutes | Serves 6

1 tablespoon oil
2 pounds beef chuck roast, cut into cubes
Salt and pepper
1 tablespoon chili powder
2 tablespoons cumin powder
1 tablespoon paprika
1 cup beef broth
8 ounces (227 g) Portobello mushrooms, chopped
1 tablespoon onion powder
1 can tomato paste
1 can crushed tomatoes

1. Press the Sauté button on the Instant Pot.
2. Heat the oil and sauté the beef chuck roast until lightly golden on all sides.
3. Season with salt and pepper to taste.
4. Stir in the rest of the ingredients.
5. Close the lid and press the Meat/Stew button.
6. Adjust the cooking time to 60 minutes.
7. Do natural pressure release.

Poor Man's Pot Roast

Prep time: 10 minutes | Cook time: 60 minutes | Serves 8

1 tablespoon olive oil
1 onion, chopped
3 cloves of garlic
3-pound (1.4 kg) beef pot roast
1 bag frozen vegetables of your choice
1 cup beef broth
Salt and pepper

1. Press the Sauté button on the Instant Pot.
2. Heat the oil and sauté the onions and garlic.
3. Stir in the beef pot roast and sear all sides until lightly golden.
4. Stir in the rest of the ingredients.
5. Close the lid and press the Meat/Stew button.
6. Adjust the cooking time to 60 minutes.
7. Do natural pressure release.

Basic Braised Beef Short Ribs

Prep time: 5 minutes | Cook time: 40 minutes | Serves 12

1 tablespoon oil
1 onion, chopped
3 cloves of garlic, minced
4 pounds (1.8 kg) beef short ribs
Salt and pepper to taste
1 cup water

1. Press the Sauté button on the Instant Pot.
2. Heat the olive oil and sauté the onions.
3. Add in the short ribs and the rest of the ingredients.
4. Close the lid and press the Meat/Stew button.
5. Adjust the cooking time to 40 minutes.
6. Do natural pressure release.

Simple Bone-In Ribs

Prep time: 10 minutes | Cook time: 40 minutes | Serves 4

4 large beef short ribs
1 onion, chopped
3 cloves of garlic, minced
½ cup apple juice
1 cup beef broth
2 tablespoons tomato paste
Salt and pepper
1 tablespoon cornstarch + 2 tablespoons water

1. Place all ingredients except for the cornstarch slurry in the Instant Pot.
2. Close the lid and press the Meat/Stew button.
3. Adjust the cooking time to 40 minutes.
4. Do natural pressure release.
5. Once the lid is open, press the Sauté button.
6. Stir in the cornstarch slurry and allow to simmer until the sauce thickens.

Sweet and Sour Meatloaf

Prep time: 10 minutes | Cook time: 30 minutes | Serves 5

3 tablespoons sugar-free ketchup
1 tablespoon honey
1 tablespoon apple cider vinegar
2 dried bay leaves
1 pound ground beef
¼ cup finely chopped onions
½ green bell pepper, chopped
½ cup ground pork rinds
1 large egg
1 tablespoon Italian seasoning
½ teaspoon sea salt
½ teaspoon freshly ground black pepper

1. Place a trivet in the pot and pour in 1½ cups of water. On top of the trivet, place a 12-inch square of aluminum foil with the edges folded upward along the curves of the pot.
2. In a small bowl, stir together the ketchup, honey, and vinegar. Add the bay leaves. Set aside.
3. In a large bowl, combine the beef, onions, bell pepper, pork rinds, egg, Italian seasoning, salt, and black pepper. Mix with your hands to combine well, then shape the meatloaf mixture into a 6- to 7-inch loaf that will fit in the Instant Pot. Place it on the foil. Pour the ketchup mixture over the top.
4. Secure the lid and seal the vent. Select Pressure Cook or Manual and cook on high pressure for 30 minutes, then allow the pressure to naturally release for 10 minutes. Quick release the remaining pressure in the pot and remove the lid.
5. Remove the bay leaves. Carefully lift the foil from the Instant Pot to remove the meatloaf. Serve and enjoy!

Creamy Cheese Stew Beef

Prep time: 15 minutes | Cook time: 45 minutes | Serves 9

3 pounds (1.4 kg) beef shoulder, cut
    into chunks
Salt and pepper, to taste
½ teaspoon marjoram
1 tablespoon dried basil
1 tablespoon oregano
1 teaspoon dill
1 onion, sliced
5 cloves of garlic, minced
1 cup beef broth
½ cup sun-dried tomatoes
1 teaspoon red wine vinegar
½ cup feta cheese, crumbled

1. Place all ingredients in the Instant Pot except for the feta cheese. Close the lid and press the Meat/Stew button.
2. Adjust the cooking time to 45 minutes. Do natural pressure release. Once the lid is open, garnish with feta cheese on top.

Coke Beef Stew

Prep time: 15 minutes | Cook time: 45 minutes | Serves 9

2 tablespoons oil
1 onion, chopped
5 cloves of garlic, minced
3 pounds (1.4 kg) beef stew meat,
    cut into chunks
Salt and pepper, to taste
1 packet ranch dressing powder
½ cup beef broth
1 cup cola your favorite brand
1 tablespoon cornstarch + 2 tablespoons water

1. Press the Sauté button on the Instant Pot. Heat the oil and sauté the garlic and onions until fragrant.
2. Add the beef stew meat and sear all sides until lightly brown. Season with salt and pepper to taste.
3. Stir in the ranch dressing, broth, and cola. Close the lid and press the Meat/Stew button.
4. Adjust the cooking time to 45 minutes. Do natural pressure release.
5. Once the lid is open, press the Sauté button and add in the cornstarch slurry. Allow simmering until the sauce thickens.

Cheese Steak with Mushroom

Prep time: 10 minutes | Cook time: 45 minutes | Serves 8

1 tablespoon oil
2 onions, sliced
3 pounds (1.4 kg) beef chuck roast, cut into chunks
2 green peppers, sliced
2 tablespoons steak seasoning
8 ounces (227 g) mushrooms, sliced
1 cup beef stock
Salt and pepper, to taste
1 cup mozzarella cheese

1. Press the Sauté button on the Instant Pot.
2. Heat the oil and sauté the onions and beef chunks. Stir until the beef has seared on all sides. Add the green peppers, steak seasoning, mushrooms, and beef stock.
3. Season with salt and pepper to taste. Stir until well combined. Add in mozzarella cheese on top.
4. Close the lid and press the Meat/Stew button. Adjust the cooking time to 45 minutes. Do natural pressure release.

Roasted Beef with different vinegar

Prep time: 15 minutes | Cook time: 45 minutes | Serves 9

2 cups water
1 cup cider vinegar
1 cup red wine vinegar
1 onion, chopped
1 carrot, chopped
2 bay leaves
6 whole cloves
½ teaspoon ground mustard
3 pounds (1.4 kg) beef chuck roast, cut into chunks
⅓ cup sugar

1. Place all ingredients in the Instant Pot except for the feta cheese.
2. Close the lid and press the Meat/Stew button. Adjust the cooking time to 45 minutes.
3. Do natural pressure release.

Roasted Chunky Beef with Tomato Sauce

Prep time: 15 minutes | Cook time: 60 minutes | Serves 6

1 tablespoon oil
2 pounds beef chuck roast, cut into cubes
Salt and pepper, to taste
1 tablespoon chili powder
2 tablespoons cumin powder
1 tablespoon paprika
1 cup beef broth
8 ounces (227 g) Portobello mushrooms, chopped
1 tablespoon onion powder
1 can tomato paste
1 can crushed tomatoes

1. Press the Sauté button on the Instant Pot. Heat the oil and sauté the beef chuck roast until lightly golden on all sides.
2. Season with salt and pepper to taste. Stir in the rest of the ingredients. Close the lid and press the Meat/Stew button. Adjust the cooking time to 60 minutes.
3. Do natural pressure release.

Roasted Ginger-Chili Beef Chuck

Prep time: 15 minutes | Cook time: 45 minutes | Serves 4

2 tablespoons ground coffee
2 tablespoons smoked paprika
1 tablespoon black pepper
1 teaspoon salt
1 tablespoon cocoa powder
1 teaspoon chili powder
1 teaspoon ground ginger

2 pounds (907 g) beef chuck roast cut into cubes
1 cup beef broth
1 onion, chopped
6 dried figs, chopped
2 tablespoons balsamic vinegar

1. In a mixing bowl, combine the first 7 ingredients.
2. Rub this spice mixture all over the beef and allow marinating in the fridge for 30 minutes. Place the marinated beef in the Instant Pot and pour in the rest of the ingredients.
3. Close the lid and press the Meat/Stew button. Adjust the cooking time to 45 minutes. Do natural pressure release.

Pot Roast Mix Veggies

Prep time: 10 minutes | Cook time: 60 minutes | Serves 8

1 tablespoon olive oil
1 onion, chopped
3 cloves of garlic
3-pound (1.4 kg) beef pot roast
1 bag frozen vegetables of your choice
1 cup beef broth
Salt and pepper, to taste

1. Press the Sauté button on the Instant Pot.
2. Heat the oil and sauté the onions and garlic. Stir in the beef pot roast and sear all sides until lightly golden.
3. Stir in the rest of the ingredients. Close the lid and press the Meat/Stew button.
4. Adjust the cooking time to 60 minutes. Do natural pressure release.

Italian Short Ribs with Pasta Sauce

Prep time: 10 minutes | Cook time: 60 minutes | Serves 8

2 tablespoons olive oil
1 ½ cups leeks, chopped
3 pounds (1.4 kg) short-ribs, bone in
1 teaspoon Italian seasoning
Salt and pepper, to taste
½ cup dry white wine
1 ¼ cups pasta sauce

1. Press the Sauté button on the Instant Pot.
2. Heat the olive oil and sauté the leeks. Add in the short ribs and the rest of the ingredients.
3. Close the lid and press the Meat/Stew button. Adjust the cooking time to 60 minutes. Do natural pressure release.

Guinness Beer Beef Stew

Prep time: 10 minutes | Cook time: 45 minutes | Serves 4

1-pound (454 g) beef stew meat
1 ½ carrots, chopped
1 onion, chopped
4 cloves of garlic, minced
4 potatoes, diced
3 tablespoons paprika
Salt and pepper, to taste
1 cup Guinness beer
1 cup beef broth

1. Place all ingredients in the Instant Pot.
2. Close the lid and press the Meat/Stew button. Adjust the cooking time to 45 minutes. Do natural pressure release.

Chapter 8 Pork

Citrus Cinnamon Pork

Prep time: 10 minutes | Cook time: 35 minutes | Serves 4

4 pork chops
3 garlic cloves, minced
1 tablespoon cinnamon powder
Juice of 1 orange
A pinch of salt and black pepper
1 tablespoon ginger, grated
½ cup beef stock
1 teaspoon rosemary, dried

1. In your instant pot, combine all the ingredients, put the lid on and cook on High for 35 minutes.
2. Release the pressure naturally for 10 minutes, divide the mix between plates and serve.

Pork Shoulder with Apple-Broccoli Slaw

Prep time: 15 minutes | Cook time: 2 hour | Serves 8

3 pounds (1.4 kg) Whole30-compliant boneless pork shoulder, trimmed and cut into 3 portions
1¼ teaspoons salt
½ teaspoon black pepper
2 tablespoons olive oil
1 cup Whole30-compliant chicken broth
4 cloves garlic, minced
1 tablespoon chili powder
1 teaspoon ground coriander
1 teaspoon ground cumin
¾ cup Whole30-compliant avocado mayonnaise
3 tablespoons cider vinegar
1 (14-ounce / 397-g) package broccoli slaw mix
1 large tart apple, cored and cut into matchsticks
1 tablespoon fresh lime juice

1. Season the pork with 1 teaspoon of the salt and the pepper. On a 6-quart Instant Pot, select Sauté and adjust to Normal/Medium. Add the oil to the pot. When it's hot, add the pork and cook, turning occasionally, until browned, about 10 minutes. Transfer the pork to a bowl. Add the broth and garlic to the pot, stirring to scrape any browned bits from the bottom. Select Cancel.
2. Season the browned pork with the chili powder, coriander, and cumin. Return the pork to the pot. Lock the lid in place.
3. Select Manual and cook on high pressure for 60 minutes. Use natural release. Transfer to a bowl.
4. Meanwhile for the slaw, in a medium bowl, stir together the mayonnaise, vinegar, and remaining ¼ teaspoon salt. Stir in the broccoli slaw mix and apple. Cover and refrigerate until serving.
5. Use two forks to shred the pork. Drizzle the pork with 1 cup of the cooking liquid and the lime juice and toss to combine. Serve the pork with the slaw.

Pork Tenderloin Lettuce Wraps

Prep time: 15 minutes | Cook time: 25 minutes | Makes 2 dozen

3 garlic cloves, minced
1 tablespoon chili powder
1 teaspoon salt
½ teaspoon pumpkin pie spice
½ teaspoon ground cumin
½ teaspoon pepper
2 (1-pound / 454-g) pork tenderloins
1 large onion, chopped

1. Mix garlic and seasonings; rub over pork. Transfer to a 6-qt. electric pressure cooker. Add onion, apple, sweet pepper, tomatoes and water. Lock lid; make sure vent is closed. Select manual setting; adjust pressure to high and set time for 25 minutes. When finished cooking, allow pressure to naturally release for 10 minutes and then quick-release any remaining pressure according to manufacturer's instructions.
2. Remove pork; cool slightly. Shred meat into bite-size pieces; return to pressure cooker.
3. Select saute setting and adjust for low heat. Stir in raisins and olives; heat through. Serve in lettuce leaves; sprinkle with slivered almonds.

1 small Granny Smith apple, peeled and chopped
1 small sweet red pepper, chopped
1 (10-ounce / 283-g) can diced tomatoes and green chilies, undrained
1 cup water
½ cup golden raisins
½ cup chopped pimiento-stuffed olives
24 Bibb or Boston lettuce leaves
¼ cup slivered almonds, toasted

Pork Shoulder Chili and Celery

Prep time: 10 minutes | Cook time: 30 minutes | Serves 4

2 pounds (907 g) pork shoulder, boneless and cubed
2 tablespoons avocado oil
A pinch of salt and black pepper
2 tablespoons chili powder
2 celery stalks, chopped
4 garlic cloves, minced
1½ cups beef stock
1 tablespoon sage, chopped

1. Set your instant pot on Sauté mode, add the oil, heat it up, add the garlic and cook for 2 minutes.
2. Add the meat and brown for 3 minutes more.
3. Add the rest of the ingredients, put the lid on and cook on High for 25 minutes.
4. Release the pressure naturally for 10 minutes, divide everything between plates and serve.

Ranch Boneless Pork Chops

Prep time: 5 minutes | Cook time: 7 minutes | Serves 4

2 tablespoons olive oil
1 pound (454 g) thick-cut boneless pork chops
½ teaspoon salt
¼ teaspoon black pepper
1 cup chicken broth
1 (1-ounce / 28-g) Whole30-compliant ranch seasoning packet

1. Press Sauté button on Instant Pot® and add oil. Let oil heat up 1 minute.
2. Add pork chops in a single layer and sprinkle with salt and pepper. Let cook 30 seconds and flip. Cook an additional 30 seconds.
3. In a small bowl, whisk together chicken broth and ranch seasoning. Pour in broth mixture and deglaze bottom of pot.
4. Turn Instant Pot® off.
5. Close lid and set pressure release to Sealing.
6. Press Manual or Pressure Cook button and adjust time to 5 minutes.
7. When the timer beeps, allow pressure to release naturally and then unlock lid and remove it.
8. Serve hot.

Peperonata with Pork Sausages with Olives

Prep time: 10 minutes | Cook time: 8 minutes | Serves 4

1 teaspoon olive oil
8 pork sausages, casing removed
1 green bell pepper, seeded and sliced
1 red bell pepper, seeded and sliced
1 jalapeño pepper, seeded and sliced
1 red onion, chopped
2 garlic cloves, minced
2 Roma tomatoes, puréed
1 cup roasted vegetable broth
1 tablespoon Italian seasoning
2 tablespoons fresh Italian parsley
2 tablespoons ripe olives, pitted and sliced

1. Press the "Sauté" button to heat up the Instant Pot. Once hot, add the oil; sear your sausages until no longer pink in center.
2. Add the other ingredients, except for the olives and parsley; stir to combine well.
3. Secure the lid. Choose the "Manual" setting and cook for 8 minutes at High pressure. Once cooking is complete, use a quick pressure release; carefully remove the lid.
4. Serve garnished with fresh parsley and olives. Bon appétit!

Pork Char Siu with Vegetable Medley

Prep time: 25 minutes | Cook time: 40 minutes | Serves 4

For the Pork Char Siu:

2 tablespoons toasted sesame oil

2 pounds (907 g) (907 g) Whole30-compliant pork
  tenderloin, cut into 4-inch pieces

2 teaspoons salt

1 cup minced white onion

8 cloves garlic, minced

1 tablespoon Whole30-compliant tomato paste

1 tablespoon Whole30-compliant five-spice powder

1 cup pineapple juice

½ cup apple juice concentrate

¼ cup coconut aminos

1 tablespoon Whole30-compliant fish sauce

1 tablespoon red wine vinegar

For the Vegetable Medley:

1 tablespoon toasted sesame oil

1 tablespoon minced garlic

1 piece (1 inch) fresh ginger, peeled and minced

2 green onions, sliced

1 cup shredded cabbage

1 cup broccoli florets

4 cups cauliflower florets

2 tablespoons coconut aminos

½ teaspoon salt

2 large eggs, lightly beaten

1. Make the char siu: On a 6-quart Instant Pot, select Sauté and adjust to Normal/Medium. Add the sesame oil to the pot. When it's hot, add the pork and salt. Cook, stirring occasionally, until browned on all sides, about 5 minutes. Transfer the pork to a medium bowl; set aside. Add the onion and garlic to the pot. Cook, stirring occasionally, until lightly golden, about 5 minutes. Add the tomato paste and five-spice powder. Cook, stirring, for 1 minute. Press Cancel. Add the pineapple juice, apple juice concentrate, coconut aminos, fish sauce, and vinegar. Return the pork to the pot.
2. Lock the lid in place. Select Manual and cook on high pressure for 15 minutes. Use quick release. Transfer the pork to a platter; cover to keep warm.
3. On the Instant Pot, select Sauté and adjust to Normal/Medium. Bring the sauce to a simmer. Cook, stirring occasionally, until the sauce is reduced by half, 15 to 20 minutes.
4. Make the vegetable medley: Meanwhile, heat the sesame oil in an extra-large skillet over medium-high heat. Add the garlic, ginger, and green onions. Cook, stirring, until the garlic is lightly browned, about 30 seconds. Add the cabbage, broccoli, and cauliflower and cook, stirring, for 8 to 10 minutes. Add the coconut aminos, salt, and 2 tablespoons water. When the water has evaporated, move the vegetables to one side of the pan. Add the eggs to the empty side and cook, stirring frequently, to scramble the eggs, 1 to 2 minutes. Stir the eggs into the vegetables.
5. Serve the sauce over the pork with the vegetable medley alongside.

Cocoa Pork Chops

Prep time: 10 minutes | Cook time: 30 minutes | Serves 4

4 pork chops

A pinch of salt and black pepper

2 tablespoons Whole30-compliant cocoa
  powder

2 tablespoons hot sauce

1 cup beef stock

2 teaspoons chili powder

¼ teaspoon cumin, ground

1 tablespoon parsley, chopped

1. In your instant pot, combine the pork chops with the rest of the ingredients, put the lid on and cook on High for 30 minutes.
2. Release the pressure naturally for 10 minutes, divide the mix between plates and serve with a side salad.

Pork Sausage Loaf with Gremolata

Prep time: 15 minutes | Cook time: 29 minutes | Serves 6

1 large egg, lightly beaten

1 stalk celery, finely chopped

½ cup finely chopped onion

⅓ cup finely chopped dried apricots

3 cloves garlic, minced

1 teaspoon dried sage, crushed

½ teaspoon fennel seeds, crushed

⅛ teaspoon ground cloves

1 teaspoon salt

¾ teaspoon black pepper

1½ pounds (680 g) ground pork

1 (2¼- to 2½-pound / 1.0- to 1.1-kg) butternut squash, peeled, halved,
  seeded, and cut into 1-inch cubes

1 tablespoon clarified butter or ghee

½ cup chopped walnuts, toasted

½ cup chopped fresh parsley

1½ teaspoons grated orange zest

1. In a large bowl, combine the egg, celery, onion, apricots, garlic, sage, fennel seeds, cloves, ½ teaspoon of the salt, and ½ teaspoon of the pepper. Add the pork; mix well. On a 12 x 18-inch piece of foil, shape the meat mixture into an 8-inch-long loaf. Place in the center of the foil. Wrap the foil around the loaf to enclose. Poke several holes on the top of the foil to allow steam to escape.
2. Place the rack in a 6-quart Instant Pot. Add 1 cup water to the pot. Place the foil packet on the rack. Lock the lid in place.
3. Select Manual and cook on high pressure for 25 minutes. Use natural release.
4. Carefully remove the foil packet and rack. Pour the water out of the pot. Return the rack to the pot. Add ¾ cup water to the pot. Place the squash on the rack. Lock the lid in place.
5. Select Manual and cook on high pressure for 4 minutes. Use quick release. Transfer the squash to a large bowl. Add the butter, remaining ½ teaspoon salt, and remaining ¼ teaspoon pepper. Use a potato masher or fork to mash the squash.
6. In a small bowl, combine the walnuts, parsley, and orange zest. Unwrap the sausage loaf and cut into 6 slices. Serve the mashed squash alongside the slices, sprinkled with the gremolata.

Pork Ribs with Collard Greens

Prep time: 20 minutes | Cook time: 1 hour | Serves 4

For the Ribs:

1½ teaspoons salt

1 teaspoon black pepper

1 teaspoon garlic powder

1 teaspoon onion powder

1 (4-pound / 1.8-kg) rack pork spareribs or baby back ribs, membrane removed and cut into 4 portions

¼ cup cider vinegar

For the Sauce:

½ cup Whole30-compliant avocado mayonnaise

2 tablespoons cider vinegar

½ teaspoon Whole30-compliant hot sauce

½ teaspoon coconut aminos

¼ teaspoon onion powder

¼ teaspoon garlic powder

⅛ teaspoon salt

⅛ teaspoon black pepper

For the Collard Greens:

2 tablespoons extra-virgin olive oil

2 cloves garlic, minced

1 (1-pound / 454-g) bag cleaned and chopped collard greens or 2 bunches collard greens, stemmed and chopped

1 tablespoon cider vinegar

½ teaspoon salt

¼ teaspoon red pepper flakes

Make the Ribs
1. In a small bowl, combine the salt, pepper, garlic powder, and onion powder. Sprinkle over the ribs. In a 6-quart Instant Pot, combine 1 cup water and the vinegar. Add the rack and place the ribs on the rack. Lock the lid in place.
2. Select Manual and cook on high pressure for 20 minutes. Use natural pressure for 10 minutes, then quick release the remaining pressure. Remove the rack and discard the cooking liquid.

Make the Sauce
3. Meanwhile, in a small bowl, whisk together the mayonnaise, vinegar, hot sauce, coconut aminos, onion powder, garlic powder, salt, and pepper.
4. Preheat the broiler. Place the ribs on a foil-lined large rimmed baking sheet, meaty sides up. Spoon the sauce on the ribs. Broil until bubbly and starting to brown, about 3 minutes.

Make the Collard Greens
5. On the Instant Pot, select Sauté and adjust to Normal/Medium. Add the olive oil. When it's hot, add the garlic and cook, stirring, for 30 seconds. Add the collard greens. Use tongs to toss the greens with the oil and garlic. Press Cancel. Add 1 cup of water to the pot. Lock the lid in place.
6. Select Manual and cook on high pressure for 3 minutes. Use quick release. Drain and discard the liquid. Use tongs to transfer the collard greens to a bowl. Toss with the vinegar, salt, and red pepper flakes. Serve the ribs with the collard greens.

Pork Shoulder with Brussels Sprouts

Prep time: 5 minutes | Cook time: 30 minutes | Serves 4

2 pounds (907 g) pork shoulder, cubed

1½ cups beef stock

2 cups Brussels sprouts, trimmed and halved

2 tablespoons olive oil

1 tablespoon parsley, chopped

1 tablespoon sweet paprika

1. Set your instant pot on Sauté mode, add the oil, heat it up, add the meat and brown for 5 minutes.
2. Add the rest of the ingredients, put the lid on and cook on High for 25 minutes.
3. Release the pressure naturally for 10 minutes, divide the mix between plates and serve.

Pork with Salsa Sauce and Avocado

Prep time: 20 minutes | Cook time: 12 minutes | Serves 8

2 teaspoons grapeseed oil
3 pounds (1.4 kg) pork tenderloin, cut into slices
½ teaspoon dried thyme
½ teaspoon dried marjoram
1 teaspoon ground cumin
1 teaspoon paprika
Sea salt and ground black pepper, to taste
1 teaspoon granulated garlic
1 cup water
1 avocado, pitted, peeled and sliced

For the Salsa Sauce:
1 cup pureed tomatoes
2 bell peppers, deveined and chopped
1 teaspoon granulated garlic
1 minced jalapeño, chopped
1 cup onion, chopped
2 tablespoons fresh cilantro, minced
3 teaspoons lime juice

1. Press the "Sauté" button to heat up the Instant Pot. Once hot, add the oil; sear the pork until delicately browned on all sides.
2. Add the seasonings, garlic, and water to the Instant Pot.
3. Secure the lid. Choose the "Manual" setting and cook for 12 minutes at High pressure. Once cooking is complete, use a natural pressure release; carefully remove the lid.
4. Shred the pork with two forks and reserve.
5. In a mixing bowl, thoroughly combine all salsa ingredients. Spoon the salsa mixture over the prepared pork. Garnish with avocado slices and serve. Bon appétit!

Cajun Pork Chops

Prep time: 10 minutes | Cook time: 30 minutes | Serves 4

1½ pounds (680 g) pork chops
1 pound (454 g) Brussels sprouts, trimmed and halved
2 tablespoons Whole30-compliant Cajun seasoning
1 cup beef stock
A pinch of salt and black pepper
1 tablespoon parsley, chopped

1. In your instant pot, combine all the ingredients, put the lid on and cook on High for 30 minutes.
2. Release the pressure naturally for 10 minutes, divide everything between plates and serve.

Porchetta

Prep time: 10 minutes | Cook time: 20 minutes | Serves 4

3 tablespoons extra-virgin olive oil
4 cloves garlic, minced
1 tablespoon fennel seeds
½ teaspoon dried thyme
½ teaspoon dried rosemary
1¼ teaspoons salt
1 (1½ pound / 680-g) Whole30-compliant pork tenderloin, fat trimmed
6 slices Whole30-compliant bacon
1 (9-ounce / 255-g) package shaved Brussels sprouts
2 medium shallots, sliced
¼ teaspoon coarse black pepper

1. Place the rack in a 6-quart Instant Pot. Add 1 cup water to the pot.
2. Using a mortar and pestle, combine 1 tablespoon of the olive oil, the garlic, fennel seeds, thyme, rosemary, and 1 teaspoon of the salt until a paste forms. Rub the paste all over the pork. Tuck the small end under. Wrap the bacon around the tenderloin. Place the tenderloin on the rack. Lock the lid in place.
3. Select Manual and cook on high pressure for 15 minutes. Use natural release. Remove the pork from the pot; cover with foil to keep warm. Discard the cooking liquid.
4. On the Instant Pot, select Sauté and adjust to More/High. Add the remaining 2 tablespoons olive oil. When it's hot, add the Brussels sprouts, shallots, and remaining ¼ teaspoon salt. Cook until tender, 4 to 6 minutes. Sprinkle with coarse black pepper.
5. Slice the tenderloin and serve with the Brussels sprouts.

Jamaican Pork Shoulder

Prep time: 5 minutes | Cook time: 53 minutes | Serves 6

2 pounds (907 g) pork shoulder
¼ cup beef broth
¾ tablespoon olive oil
¼ cup Jamaican jerk spice blend

1. Use Jamaican jerk spice with olive oil to marinate the pork for 10 minutes,
2. Select the Sauté function on the instant pot and place the marinated pork inside,
3. Sear each side for 4 minutes then add the broth.
4. Secure the lid and cook for 45 minutes at high pressure on the Manual setting.
5. Natural release the steam for 10 minutes then remove the lid. Serve hot.

Pork Roast and Balsamic Asparagus

Prep time: 10 minutes | Cook time: 27 minutes | Serves 4

2 pounds (907 g) pork roast
4 garlic cloves, minced
1 yellow onions, chopped
1 cup beef stock
1 bunch asparagus, trimmed
2 tablespoons balsamic vinegar
A pinch of salt and black pepper
1 teaspoon smoked paprika
1 tablespoon basil, chopped
1 teaspoon chives, chopped
1 tablespoon olive oil

1. Set your instant pot on sauté mode, add the oil, heat it up, add the onion and garlic and sauté for 2 minutes.
2. Add the meat and brown for 5 minutes more.
3. Add the stock, salt, pepper and the basil, put the lid on and cook on High for 20 minutes.
4. Release the pressure naturally for 10 minutes, set the pot on sauté mode again, add the asparagus, vinegar and the chives, cook for 7 minutes more, divide everything between plates and serve.

Chinese Five-Spice Pork Ribs

Prep time: 15 minutes | Cook time: 30 minutes | Serves 4

2 tablespoons coconut oil
3 pounds (1.4 kg) pork baby back ribs, cut into 3 portions
1 tablespoon Whole30-compliant five-spice powder
½ teaspoon paprika
½ teaspoon ground coriander
1 teaspoon Primal Palate curry powder or other Whole30-compliant curry powder
2 cups water or Whole30-compliant chicken broth
1 (10-ounce / 283-g) package frozen roasted cauliflower or about 4 cups cauliflower florets, roasted
⅓ cup coconut aminos
2 teaspoons toasted sesame oil
½ teaspoon ground ginger
¼ teaspoon granulated garlic
½ teaspoon Himalayan pink salt
Chopped fresh parsley, for garnish

1. In a large cast-iron skillet, heat the coconut oil over medium-high heat. Add the ribs, meaty sides down, and cook until browned, about 4 minutes. Season the ribs with the five-spice powder, paprika, coriander, and curry powder.
2. Meanwhile, place the rack in a 6-quart Instant Pot. Add the water or broth.
3. Place the ribs on the rack. Lock the lid in place. Select Manual and cook on high pressure for 20 minutes. Use natural release for 10 minutes, then quick release.
4. Meanwhile, prepare the cauliflower according to the package directions. Preheat the oven to 400°F (205°C).
5. In a small bowl, stir together the coconut aminos, sesame oil, ginger, and granulated garlic. Place the ribs on a foil-lined rimmed baking sheet and brush with the some of the sauce. Sprinkle with the salt. Bake for 10 minutes, brushing with the remaining sauce after the first 5 minutes. Cut into the ribs and sprinkle with parsley. Serve with the cauliflower.

Pork and Tarragon Mix

Prep time: 10 minutes | Cook time: 30 minutes | Serves 4

1 red onion, chopped
1 tablespoon tarragon, chopped
½ teaspoon oregano, dried
A pinch of salt and black pepper
1½ pounds (680 g) pork stew meat, cubed
1 tablespoon olive oil
1 cup tomato puree

1. Set the instant pot on Sauté mode, add the oil, heat it up, add the meat and the onion and brown for 5 minutes.
2. Add the rest of the ingredients, put the lid on and cook on High for 25 minutes.
3. Release the pressure naturally for 10 minutes, divide the mix between plates and serve.

Pork Loin Chops with Mushroom

Prep time: 15 minutes | Cook time: 15 minutes | Serves 4

4 tablespoons clarified butter or ghee
2 (8-ounce / 227-g) packages sliced cremini
    mushrooms
½ cup sliced yellow onion
2 cloves garlic, minced
¾ teaspoon salt
1¼ cups Whole30-compliant chicken broth
4 Whole30-compliant bone-in, 1-inch-thick
    pork loin chops (2-pound / 907-g total)
½ teaspoon dried thyme
¼ teaspoon black pepper
2 tablespoons arrowroot powder
1 pound (454 g) broccoli florets
1 teaspoon fresh lemon juice
4 slices Whole30-compliant bacon, crisp-
    cooked and crumbled

1. On a 6-quart Instant Pot, select Sauté and adjust to Normal/Medium. Add 2 tablespoons of the butter to the pot. When it's hot, add the mushrooms, onion, garlic, and ½ teaspoon of the salt and cook, stirring occasionally, until the vegetables are browned and tender, 6 to 8 minutes. Select Cancel. Stir in 1 cup of the broth. Sprinkle the pork chops with the thyme and pepper; add to the pot. Lock the lid in place.
2. Select Manual and cook on high pressure for 4 minutes. Use quick release. Transfer the pork chops to a serving platter; cover to keep warm.
3. In a small bowl, whisk together the arrowroot and remaining ¼ cup broth. Add the arrowroot mixture to the pot. Select Sauté and adjust to Normal/Medium. Cook until the sauce comes to a simmer. Select Cancel.
4. Place the broccoli florets in a microwave-safe dish and add 3 tablespoons water. Cover and microwave, stirring once, until tender, about 5 minutes. Stir in the lemon juice, remaining 2 tablespoons butter, and remaining ¼ teaspoon salt.
5. Serve the mushroom sauce over the pork chops and top with the bacon. Serve the broccoli alongside.

Pork Chops with Bell Peppers

Prep time: 10 minutes | Cook time: 35 minutes | Serves 4

2 tablespoons olive oil
4 pork chops
A pinch of salt and black pepper
1 red bell pepper, roughly chopped
1 green bell pepper, roughly chopped
3 garlic cloves, minced
1 red onion, chopped
2 cups beef stock
1 tablespoon parsley, chopped

1. Set your instant pot on Sauté mode, add the oil, heat it up, add the pork chops and brown for 2 minutes.
2. Add the garlic and the onion and brown for 3 minutes more.
3. Add all the other ingredients except the parsley, put the lid on and cook on High for 30 minutes.
4. Release the pressure naturally for 10 minutes, divide the mix between plates, sprinkle the parsley on top and serve.

Italian Pork Tenderloin

Prep time: 10 minutes | Cook time: 25 minutes | Serves 4

2 teaspoons olive oil
3 cloves garlic, minced
2 teaspoons Italian seasoning
1 teaspoon coarse salt

½ teaspoon freshly ground black pepper
1½ pounds (680 g) pork tenderloin
1 cup water or chicken stock

1. In a small bowl, mix together the olive oil, garlic, Italian seasoning, salt and pepper. Rub the mixture all over the outside of the pork loin.
2. Pour the water or stock into the Instant Pot and insert the steam trivet. Place the pork loin on the trivet. Secure the lid with the steam vent in the sealed position. Press manual and immediately adjust the timer to 25 minutes. Check that the display light is beneath high pressure.
3. Once the timer sounds, allow the pressure to release naturally for 5 minutes, then quick release the pressure and carefully remove the lid. Remove the pork and allow it to rest on a carving board for 5 minutes, then slice and serve.

Nutmeg Pork with Parsley

Prep time: 10 minutes | Cook time: 30 minutes | Serves 4

1½ pounds (680 g) pork meat, cubed
2 tablespoons parsley, chopped
2 garlic cloves, minced
A pinch of salt and black pepper
1 cup beef stock
2 teaspoons nutmeg, ground
½ teaspoon sweet paprika
2 tablespoons olive oil

1. Set the instant pot on Sauté mode, add the oil, heat it up, add the meat and garlic and brown for 5 minutes.
2. Add the rest of the ingredients, put the lid on and cook on High for 25 minutes.
3. Release the pressure naturally for 10 minutes, divide everything between plates and serve.

Chili Pork Roast

Prep time: 10 minutes | Cook time: 35 minutes | Serves 4

1 yellow onion, chopped
1½ pounds pork roast
12 ounces (340 g) tomatoes, crushed
4 garlic cloves, minced
2 tablespoons chili powder
1 teaspoon oregano, dried
1 tablespoon olive oil
A pinch of salt and black pepper
1 tablespoon apple cider vinegar
1 cup beef stock

1. Set the instant pot on sauté mode, add the oil, heat it up, add the onion and garlic and sauté for 5 minutes.
2. Add the meat and the rest of the ingredients, put the lid on and cook on High for 30 minutes.
3. Release the pressure naturally for 10 minutes, divide the mix between plates and serve.

Pork Chops and Cherry Sauce

Prep time: 10 minutes | Cook time: 22 minutes | Serves 4

4 pork chops
A pinch of salt and black pepper
1 cup beef stock
1 cup cherries, pitted
1 tablespoon parsley, chopped
1 tablespoon balsamic vinegar
1 tablespoon avocado oil

1. Set the instant pot on Sauté mode, add the oil, heat it up, add the pork chops and brown for 2 minutes on each side.
2. Add the rest of the ingredients, put the lid on and cook on High for 20 minutes.
3. Release the pressure fast for 5 minutes, divide everything between plates and serve.

Pork Meatloaf with Boiled Eggs

Prep time: 10 minutes | Cook time: 25 minutes | Serves 6

1 tablespoon avocado oil
1½ cup ground pork
1 teaspoon chives
1 teaspoon salt
½ teaspoon ground black pepper
2 tablespoons coconut flour
3 eggs, hard-boiled, peeled
1 cup water

1. Brush a loaf pan with avocado oil. In the mixing bowl, mix the ground pork, chives, salt, ground black pepper, and coconut flour.
2. Transfer the mixture in the loaf pan and flatten with a spatula.
3. Fill the meatloaf with hard-boiled eggs.
4. Pour water and insert the trivet in the Instant Pot.
5. Lower the loaf pan over the trivet in the Instant Pot. Close the lid.
6. Select Pressure Cook mode and set cooking time for 25 minutes on High Pressure.
7. When timer beeps, use a natural pressure release for 10 minutes, then release any remaining pressure. Open the lid. Serve immediately.

Pork and Eggplant Lasagna

Prep time: 10 minutes | Cook time: 30 minutes | Serves 6

2 eggplants, sliced
1 teaspoon salt
10 ounces (283 g) ground pork
1 cup Mozzarella, shredded
1 tablespoon unsweetened tomato purée
1 teaspoon butter, softened
1 cup chicken stock

1. Sprinkle the eggplants with salt and let sit for 10 minutes, then pat dry with paper towels.
2. In a mixing bowl, mix the ground pork, butter, and tomato purée. Make a layer of the sliced eggplants in the bottom of the Instant Pot and top with ground pork mixture.
3. Top the ground pork with Mozzarella and repeat with remaining ingredients.
4. Pour in the chicken stock. Close the lid. Select Pressure Cook mode and set cooking time for 30 minutes on High Pressure.
5. When timer beeps, use a natural pressure release for 10 minutes, then release the remaining pressure and open the lid.
6. Cool for 10 minutes and serve.

Chapter 9 Fish and Seafood

Lemon Salmon Fillets

Prep time: 5 minutes | Cook time: 3 minutes | Serves 3

1 (5-ounce / 142-g) salmon fillet
1 cup water
3 lemon slices
1 teaspoon fresh lemon juice
Fresh cilantro, for garnish
Salt and ground black pepper, to taste

1. Add the water to the Instant pot and place a trivet inside,
2. In a shallow bowl; place the salmon fillet. Sprinkle salt and pepper over it.
3. Squeeze some lemon juice on top then place a lemon slice over the salmon fillet.
4. Cover the lid and lock it. Set its pressure release handle to Sealing position.
5. Use Steam function on your cooker for 3 minutes to cook.
6. When it beeps; do a Quick release and release the steam. Remove the lid then serve with the lemon slice and fresh cilantro on top.

Sardines in Tomato Puree

Prep time: 10 minutes | Cook time: 8 hours | Serves 4

1 tablespoon olive oil
1 pound (454 g) fresh sardines, cubed
2 plum tomatoes, chopped finely
½ large onion, sliced
1 garlic clove, minced
½ cup tomato puree
Salt and ground black pepper, to taste

1. Select the "Sauté" function on your Instant pot then add the oil and sardines to it.
2. Let it sauté for 2 minutes then add all the remaining ingredients.
3. Cover the lid and select "Slow cook" function for 8 hours.
4. Remove the lid and stir the cooked curry.
5. Serve warm.

Tilapia Fillet with Pineapple Salsa

Prep time: 5 minutes | Cook time: 2 minutes | Serves 4

1 pound (454 g) tilapia fillets
¼ teaspoon salt
⅛ teaspoon black pepper
½ cup pineapple salsa
1 cup water

1. Place tilapia in the center of a 1½' piece of foil. Season tilapia with salt and pepper.
2. Fold foil up on all sides to resemble a bowl and pour in salsa. Fold foil over top of tilapia and crimp edges.
3. Place trivet and water in Instant Pot®. Carefully place foil packet on top of trivet.
4. Close lid and set pressure release to Sealing.
5. Press Manual or Pressure Cook button and adjust time to 2 minutes.
6. When the timer beeps, quick release pressure and then unlock lid and remove it.
7. Remove foil packet from Instant Pot®. Carefully open foil packet; steam will release from inside.
8. Serve tilapia with salsa as garnish.

Tuna and Tomato Chowder

Prep time: 10 minutes | Cook time: 7 hours | Serves 3

6 ounces (170 g) water-packed tuna drained chunks
1 (8-ounce / 227-g) can diced tomatoes with juice
1 chopped medium red potato
½ teaspoon cayenne pepper
½ teaspoon freshly ground black pepper
½ teaspoon crushed dried thyme
½ cup chopped celery
½ cup chopped onion
½ cup peeled and roughly shredded carrot
7 ounces (198 g) chicken broth
Salt, to taste

1. Add all the Ingredients except tuna to Instant Pot and mix them well.
2. Secure the lid with its pressure release handle on the venting position.
3. Select the Slow Cook function with Medium heat for 7 hours,
4. Remove the lid after 7 hours and add tuna chunks to the pot.
5. Cover the lid immediately and let tuna stay in the steaming hot gravy for 5 minutes, Serve sizzling hot chowder immediately.

Seafood and Veggie Soup

Prep time: 15 minutes | Cook time: 1¾ hours | Serves 4

1½ tablespoons olive oil
1 pound (454 g) sea scallops
½ medium onion, chopped
1 pound (454 g) mussels, cleaned and debearded
¼ cup carrot, peeled and chopped
¼ cup celery stalk, chopped
3 cups fresh spinach, chopped
8 cups chicken broth
1 garlic clove, minced
½ cup fresh parsley, chopped
½ pound (227 g) large shrimp, peeled and deveined
½ cup fresh tomatoes, chopped finely

1½ tablespoons fresh lime juice
Sea salt and ground black pepper, to taste

1. Select the "sauté" function on your Instant pot and add the oil with all the vegetables except parsley.
2. Sauté for 1 minute then add the parsley. Then secure the lid.
3. Select the "Slow Cook" for 1 hour. Keep the pressure release handle to the "Venting" position.
4. Place the shrimp, mussels, and scallops over vegetables and cover the lid.
5. Secure the lid and "Slow Cook" for another 45 minutes.
6. Serve hot.

Special Shrimp and Root Vegetable Curry

Prep time: 10 minutes | Cook time: 9 minutes | Serves 8

2 pounds (907 g) medium shrimp; peeled and deveined
2 tablespoons olive oil
1½ medium onion; chopped.
1½ teaspoons ground cumin
2 teaspoons red chili powder
2 teaspoons ground turmeric
3 medium white rose potatoes; diced
½ cup fresh cilantro; chopped.
6 medium tomatoes; chopped
½ cup water

1½ tablespoons fresh lemon juice
Salt, to taste

1. Select the Sauté function on your Instant Pot. Add the oil and onions then cook for 2 minutes,
2. Add the tomatoes, potatoes, cilantro and all the spices into the pot and secure the lid.
3. Select the Manual function at medium pressure for 5 minutes,
4. Do a natural release then remove the lid. Stir shrimp into the pot.
5. Secure the lid again then set the Manual function with high pressure for 2 minutes,
6. When it beeps; use Natural release and let it stand for 10 minutes, Remove the lid and serve hot.

Rosemary Cod and Tomato Platter

Prep time: 5 minutes | Cook time: 5 minutes | Serves 6

6 (4-ounce / 113-g) cod fillets
1½ pounds (680 g) cherry tomatoes; halved
3 garlic cloves; minced
2½ tablespoons fresh rosemary; chopped.
2 tablespoons olive oil
Salt and freshly ground black pepper, to taste

1. Add the olive oil, half of the tomatoes and rosemary to the insert of the Instant Pot.
2. Place cod fillets over these tomatoes, Then add more tomatoes to the pot.
3. Add the garlic to the pot. Then secure the lid.
4. Select the Manual function with high pressure for 5 minutes,
5. When it beeps; use the quick release to discharge all the steam. Serve cod fillets with tomatoes and sprinkle a pinch of salt and pepper on top.

Sea Scallops and Vegetable with Aioli

Prep time: 15 minutes | Cook time: 25 minutes | Serves 4

1 teaspoon ground coriander
¾ teaspoon black pepper
⅛ teaspoon ground nutmeg
1 pound (454 g) fresh or thawed frozen sea scallops
3 tablespoons extra-virgin olive oil
12 ounces (340 g) small round red potatoes, quartered
2 medium parsnips, peeled and cut crosswise into
    ½-inch-thick slices
1 medium shallot, cut into wedges
1 teaspoon coarse salt
1 medium zucchini or yellow summer squash, cut into
    1½-inch pieces
½ cup Whole30-compliant avocado mayonnaise
2 tablespoons fresh lemon juice
1 small clove garlic, minced
Pinch saffron threads, crushed (optional)
Dash coarse salt
½ cup fresh basil leaves

1. In a small bowl, combine the coriander, ¼ teaspoon of the pepper, and the nutmeg. Sprinkle the seasoning on the scallops.
2. On a 6-quart Instant Pot, select Sauté and adjust to Normal/Medium. Add 1 tablespoon of the olive oil to the pot. When it's hot, add half the scallops and cook, turning once, just until browned, 2 to 3 minutes. Transfer the scallops to a plate; cover to keep warm. Repeat with 1 tablespoon of the oil and the remaining scallops.
3. In a large bowl, combine the potatoes, parsnips, and shallot. Drizzle with the remaining 1 tablespoon oil and sprinkle with the salt and remaining ½ teaspoon pepper. Toss to coat.
4. Add ¾ cup water to the pot. Place the rack in the bottom of the pot. Add the potato mixture to the rack. Lock the lid in place.
5. Select Manual and cook on high pressure for 9 minutes. Use quick release. Arrange the scallops and zucchini in an even layer on the potato mixture. Lock the lid in place.
6. Select Manual and cook on high pressure for 1 minute. Use quick release.
7. In a small bowl, stir together the mayonnaise, lemon juice, garlic, saffron (if using), and the dash salt.
8. Sprinkle the scallops and vegetables with the basil and serve with the aioli.

Chili Lime Tilapia Fillet

Prep time: 5 minutes | Cook time: 2 minutes | Serves 4

1 cup water
4 tablespoons lime juice
3 tablespoons chili powder
½ teaspoon salt
1 pound (454 g) tilapia fillets

1. Pour water into Instant Pot® and add trivet.
2. In a small bowl, whisk together lime juice, chili powder, and salt. Brush sauce onto both sides of tilapia fillets. Place tilapia on trivet.
3. Close lid and set pressure release to Sealing.
4. Press Manual or Pressure Cook button and adjust time to 2 minutes.
5. When the timer beeps, quick release pressure and then unlock lid and remove it.
6. Serve hot.

Fresh Sardines Curry

Prep time: 10 minutes | Cook time: 8 hours | Serves 4

1 pound (454 g) fresh sardines; cubed
1 tablespoon olive oil
2 plum tomatoes; chopped finely
½ cup tomato puree
½ large onion; sliced
1 garlic clove; minced
Salt and ground black pepper, to taste

1. Select the Sauté function on your Instant pot then add oil and sardines to it.
2. Let it sauté for 2 minutes then add all the remaining ingredients,
3. Cover the lid and select Slow cook function for 8 hours,
4. Remove the lid and stir the cooked curry. Serve warm.

Seafood and Red Potato Platter

Prep time: 10 minutes | Cook time: 35 minutes | Serves 4

½ pound (227 g) medium-sized red potatoes, halved
1 cup seafood stock
1½ tablespoons Cajun's shrimp boil
½ pound (227 g) clams, fresh frozen
½ pound (227 g) shell on shrimp, deveined
½ pound (227 g) mussels, fresh or frozen
1 lemon, quartered
½ pound (227 g) smoked Kielbasa, cut into 2-inch pieces
1 tablespoon chopped parsley
Cilantro and lemon wedges, for garnish

1. Add the seafood stock, boiling spice, and potatoes to the Instant Pot.
2. Cover the lid and let it "Slow Cook" for 30 minutes till the potatoes get tender.
3. Remove the lid and add the clams, shrimp, mussels, Kielbasa, and lemon to the pot.
4. Cook for 10 minutes if you are using frozen seafood, else cook for only 5 minutes.
5. Garnish with cilantro and lemon wedges on top.
6. Serve.

Tomato-Poached Halibut Fillet

Prep time: 15 minutes | Cook time: 5 minutes | Serves 4

1 tablespoon olive oil
2 poblano peppers, finely chopped
1 small onion, finely chopped
1 can (14½-ounce / 411.1-g) fire-roasted diced tomatoes, undrained
1 can (14½-ounce / 411.1-g) no-salt-added diced tomatoes, undrained
½ cup water
¼ cup chopped pitted green olives
3 garlic cloves, minced
¼ teaspoon pepper
⅛ teaspoon salt
4 (4-ounce / 113-g) halibut fillets
⅓ cup chopped fresh cilantro
4 lemon wedges

1. Select saute setting on a 6-qt. electric pressure cooker. Adjust for medium heat; add oil. When oil is hot, cook and stir poblano peppers and onion until crisp-tender, 2 to 3 minutes. Press cancel. Stir in tomatoes, water, olives, garlic, pepper and salt. Top with fillets.
2. Lock the lid; close pressure-release valve. Adjust to pressure cook on high for 3 minutes. Quick-release pressure. A thermometer inserted in fish should read at least 145°F (63°C).
3. Sprinkle with cilantro. Serve with lemon wedges.

Fish with Lemony Ginger Sauce

Prep time: 10 minutes | Cook time: 6 minutes | Serves 4

4 white fish fillets
Juice and zest of 1 lemon
1 thumb-size ginger, grated
1 tablespoon olive oil
Salt and pepper, to taste
1 cup fish stock
4 spring onions, chopped

1. Place all ingredients except for the spring onions in the Instant Pot.
2. Close the lid and press the Manual button.
3. Adjust the cooking time to 6 minutes.
4. Do natural pressure release.
5. Once the lid is open, garnish the fish with spring onions.

Lemon and Garlic Cod Fillet

Prep time: 10 minutes | Cook time: 5 minutes | Serves 4

1 pound (454 g) cod fillets
1 medium lemon, cut into wedges
4 cloves garlic, smashed
½ teaspoon salt
¼ teaspoon black pepper
1 tablespoon olive oil
1 cup water

1. Place cod, lemon, and garlic in the center of a 1½' piece of foil. Season with salt and pepper. Drizzle with oil. Fold foil up on all sides to resemble a bowl and crimp edges tightly.
2. Place trivet and water in Instant Pot®. Carefully place foil packet on top of trivet.
3. Close lid and set pressure release to Sealing.
4. Press Manual or Pressure Cook button and adjust time to 5 minutes.
5. When the timer beeps, quick release pressure, and then unlock lid and remove it.
6. Remove foil packet from Instant Pot®. Carefully open foil packet; steam will release from inside.
7. Squeeze lemon over cod and serve.

Classic Shrimp Creole

Prep time: 10 minutes | Cook time: 7 hours | Serves 4

1 pound (454 g) shrimp (peeled and deveined)
1 (8-ounce / 227-g) can tomato sauce
1 (28-ounce / 794-g) can crush whole tomatoes
1 tablespoon olive oil
1 cup celery stalk (sliced)
¾ cup chopped white onion
½ cup green bell pepper (chopped)
½ teaspoon minced garlic
¼ teaspoon ground black pepper
1 tablespoon Worcestershire sauce
4 drops hot pepper sauce
Salt, to taste

1. Put the oil to Instant Pot along with all the Ingredients except shrimp.
2. Secure the cooker lid and keep the pressure handle valve turned to the venting position.
3. Select the Slow Cook function on your cooker and set it on medium heat.
4. Let the mixture cook for 6 hours,
5. Remove the lid afterwards and add shrimp to the pot.
6. Stir and let the shrimp cook for another 1 hour on Slow Cook function.
7. Keep the lid covered with pressure release handle in the venting position.
8. Sever immediately.

Easy Salmon Fillet

Prep time: 10 minutes | Cook time: 5 minutes | Serves 2

2 (4-ounce / 113-g) salmon fillets
½ cup homemade chicken broth
½ teaspoon lemon zest (freshly grated)
1 tablespoon fresh lemon juice
½ tablespoons olive oil
½ teaspoon garlic; minced
Salt and black pepper, to taste

1. Put all the Ingredients to the Instant pot and mix them well.
2. Secure the lid and turn its pressure release handle to Sealing position.
3. Select the Manual function at high pressure for 5 minutes,
4. When it beeps; release the steam naturally for 10 minutes,
5. Remove the lid and dish out the salmon fillets along with their sauce, Serve.

Chipotle Salmon Fillet

Prep time: 15 minutes | Cook time: 4 minutes | Serves 3 to 4

1 cup water
¾ teaspoon sea salt, divided
½ teaspoon chipotle chili powder
1 teaspoon ground cumin
3 to 4 (5-ounce / 142-g) salmon fillets with skin, about 1" thick
Juice of 2 limes
1 tablespoon white vinegar
½ cup avocado oil or olive oil
1 chipotle pepper in adobo sauce
1 tablespoon adobo sauce
¼ cup chopped fresh cilantro
Cauliflower rice, for serving

1. Pour the water into the Instant Pot and insert the steam trivet.
2. In a small bowl, combine ¼ teaspoon of the salt and the chipotle chili powder and cumin. Season the salmon with the spice mixture, rubbing it onto the fillets. Place the salmon, skin side down, on the steam trivet.
3. Secure the lid with the steam vent in the sealed position. Select steam or manual and use the plus and minus buttons to adjust the time until the display reads "4 minutes." If the salmon is thicker than 1 inch, add an additional 1 minute per ½ inch.
4. Meanwhile, make the chipotle-lime vinaigrette: In a blender or food processor, combine the lime juice, vinegar, oil, chipotle pepper, adobo sauce, cilantro and remaining ½ teaspoon of salt and blend until smooth. Set aside.
5. When the salmon is finished cooking, use a quick release. Serve the salmon over a bed of rice or cauliflower rice and pour the vinaigrette on top.

Fish Coconut Curry

Prep time: 15 minutes | Cook time: 8 minutes | Serves 4

1 tablespoons olive oil
½ teaspoon mustard seeds
1-pound (454 g) tilapia fillets, cut into thick strips
1 can coconut milk
1 tablespoon ginger, grated
15 curry leaves
½ onion, sliced
½ green pepper, sliced
½ yellow pepper, sliced
½ teaspoon turmeric powder
2 teaspoons coriander powder
1 teaspoon cumin powder
1 teaspoon garam masala
Salt and pepper

1. Press the Sauté button on the Instant Pot.
2. Heat the oil and fry the mustard seeds until they pop.
3. Pour in the rest of the ingredients.
4. Close the lid and press the Manual button.
5. Adjust the cooking time to 8 minutes.
6. Do natural pressure release.

Salmon Curry

Prep time: 15 minutes | Cook time: 12 minutes | Serves 8

3 pounds salmon fillets cut into pieces
2 tablespoon olive oil
2 Serrano peppers; chopped.
1 teaspoon ground turmeric
4 garlic cloves; minced
4 cups unsweetened coconut milk
4 curry leaves
4 teaspoon ground coriander
4 tablespoon curry powder
4 teaspoon ground cumin
2 small yellow onions; chopped.
2 teaspoon red chili powder
2 ½ cups tomatoes; chopped.
2 tablespoon fresh lemon juice
Fresh cilantro leaves Garnish

1. Put the oil and curry leaves to the insert of the Instant Pot. Select the *Sauté* function to cook for 30 secs,
2. Add the garlic and onions to the pot; cook for 5 minutes,
3. Stir in all the spices and cook for another 1 minute,
4. Put the fish, Serrano pepper, coconut milk and tomatoes while cooking.
5. Cover and lock the lid. Seal the pressure release valve,
6. Select the *Manual* function at low pressure for 5 minutes,
7. When it beeps; do a *Natural* release to release all the steam.
8. Remove the lid and squeeze in lemon juice, Garnish with fresh cilantro leaves and serve.

Delicious Cod Platter

Prep time: 10 minutes | Cook time: 5 minutes | Serves 6

6 4-ounces (113 g) cod fillets
1 ½ pounds (226 g) cherry tomatoes; halved
3 garlic cloves; minced
2 ½ tbs fresh rosemary; chopped.
2 tablespoon olive oil
Salt and freshly ground black pepper; to taste

1. Add the olive oil, half of the tomatoes and rosemary to the insert of the Instant Pot.
2. Place cod fillets over these tomatoes, Then add more tomatoes to the pot.
3. Add the garlic to the pot. Then secure the lid.
4. Select the *Manual* function with high pressure for 5 minutes,
5. When it beeps; use the quick release to discharge all the steam. Serve cod fillets with tomatoes and sprinkle a pinch of salt and pepper on top.

Sardines Curry

Prep time: 10 minutes | Cook time: 8 hours & 2 minutes | Serves 4

1 pound (454 g) fresh sardines; cubed
1 tablespoon olive oil
2 plum tomatoes; chopped finely
½ cup tomato puree
½ large onion; sliced
1 garlic clove; minced
Salt and ground black pepper; to taste

1. Select the *Sauté* function on your Instant pot then add oil and sardines to it.
2. Let it sauté for 2 minutes then add all the remaining ingredients,
3. Cover the lid and select *Slow cook* function for 8 hours,
4. Remove the lid and stir the cooked curry. Serve warm.

Zucchini Salmon Stew

Prep time: 15 minutes | Cook time: 6 hours & 10 minutes | Serves 2

½ pound (226 g) salmon fillet; cubed
½ tablespoon coconut oil
⅛ teaspoon dried oregano; crushed
⅛ teaspoon dried basil; crushed
½ medium onion; chopped.
½ garlic clove; minced
½ zucchini; sliced
½ green bell pepper; seeded and cubed
¼ cup tomatoes; chopped.
½ cup fish broth
Salt and ground black pepper; to taste

1. Add all the Ingredients to the Instant pot and mix well.
2. Secure the lid and select *Slow Cook* for 6 hrs.
3. Keep the pressure release handle to the *venting* position.
4. After complete cooking; stir the stew well. Serve immediately.

Southeast Asian Mok Pa

Prep time: 15 minutes | Cook time: 15 minutes | Serves 3

3 tablespoon sticky rice, soaked in water
1 stalk lemongrass, sliced
1 small shallot, chopped
2 cloves of garlic, minced
5 Thai bird chilies
2 tablespoons water
12 kaffir lime leaves
2 tablespoons fish sauce
1 banana leaf, washed
2 pounds (907 g)white fish fillet
1 tablespoon green onions
1 cup fresh dill leaves, chopped
½ cup cilantro leaves, chopped

1. Place in a mortar or food processor the rice, lemongrass, shallots, garlic, birth chilies, water, kaffir lime leaves, and fish sauce. Pulse until fine. Set aside.
2. Lay down the banana leaves on a leveled surface and place fish in the middle. Pour the rice mixture on top and garnish with green onions, dill, and cilantro leaves.
3. Fold the banana leaf and secure with a string. You can even wrap aluminum foil over. Place a steamer basket in the Instant Pot and pour water over.
4. Place the fish wrapped in banana leaf on the steamer rack. Close the lid and press the Steam button.
5. Adjust the cooking time to 15 minutes. Do quick pressure release.

Salmon Casserole with Mushroom Soup

Prep time: 10 minutes | Cook time: 8 hours | Serves 4

16 ounces (453 g) salmon drained and flaked

3 medium potatoes peeled and sliced

½ tablespoon olive oil

8 oz. cream of mushroom soup

¼ cup water

3 tablespoon flour

½ cup chopped scallion

¼ teaspoon ground nutmeg

Salt and freshly ground black pepper, to taste

1. Pour mushroom soup and water in a separate bowl and mix it well.
2. Add the olive oil to Instant Pot and grease it lightly.
3. Place half of the potatoes in the pot and sprinkle salt, pepper and half of the flour over it.
4. Now add a layer of half of the salmon over potatoes then a layer of half of the scallions,
5. Repeat these layers and pour mushroom soup mix on top.
6. Top it with nutmeg evenly.
7. Secure the lid and set its pressure release handle to the venting position.
8. Select the *Slow Cook* function with *Medium* heat on your Instant Pot. Let it cook for 8 hours then serve.

Steamed Lobsters with butter

Prep time: 5 minutes | Cook time: 3 minutes | Serves 4

4 pounds (1.8 kg) lobster tails; cut in half

4 tablespoons unsalted butter; melted

1 cup water

Salt, to taste

Black pepper, to taste

1. Pour 1 cup of water into the insert of Instant pot and place trivet inside it. Place all the lobster tails over the trivet with their shell side down.
2. Cover the lid and lock it. Select the *Manual* function at low pressure for 3 minutes,
3. When it beeps; press cancel and do a Quick release, Remove the lid and the trivet from the pot. Transfer the lobster to a serving plate,
4. Pour the melted butter over lobster tails to add more flavor. Sprinkle some salt and pepper on top then serve.

Garlicky Shrimp with Saffron Rice

Prep time: 10 minutes | Cook time: 8 minutes | Serves 4

1¾ cups chicken or vegetable broth

2 big pinches of saffron

3 tablespoons olive oil

1 medium yellow onion, chopped

1½ cups long-grain rice

1 cup drained canned fire-roasted tomatoes with garlic

1 cup drained, chopped roasted bell peppers

Salt and freshly ground black pepper, to taste

1 pound (454 g) frozen large/jumbo shell-on, deveined shrimp

Optional garnish:

Lemon wedges

1. In a measuring cup, combine the broth and saffron and set aside. Put the oil in the pot, select SAUTÉ, and adjust to MORE/HIGH heat.
2. When the oil is hot, add the onion and cook, stirring frequently, until tender, 4 minutes. Add the rice and stir to coat with the oil. Press CANCEL.
3. Add the broth with saffron, the tomatoes, roasted peppers, ¾ teaspoon salt, and several grinds of pepper and stir to combine. Place the frozen shrimp on top of the rice mixture, but do not stir them in.
4. Lock on the lid, select the PRESSURE COOK function, and adjust to MORE/HIGH pressure for 4 minutes. Make sure the steam valve is in the "Sealing" position.
5. When the cooking time is up, let the pressure come down naturally for 10 minutes and then quick-release the remaining pressure.
6. Gently pour the paella into a serving dish—don't stir too briskly or the rice will break up and become mushy. Serve immediately with lemon wedges on the side, if desired.

Lemony Salmon with Tomato and Curry

Prep time: 15 minutes | Cook time: 12 minutes | Serves 8

3 pounds salmon fillets cut into
    pieces
2 tablespoon olive oil
2 Serrano peppers; chopped.
1 teaspoon ground turmeric
4 garlic cloves; minced
4 cups unsweetened coconut milk
4 curry leaves
4 teaspoon ground coriander
4 tablespoon curry powder
4 teaspoon ground cumin
2 small yellow onions; chopped.
2 teaspoon red chili powder
2 ½ cups tomatoes; chopped.
2 tablespoon fresh lemon juice
Fresh cilantro leaves Garnish

1. Put the oil and curry leaves to the insert of the Instant Pot. Select the *Sauté* function to cook for 30 secs, Add the garlic and onions to the pot; cook for 5 minutes,
2. Stir in all the spices and cook for another 1 minute, Put the fish, Serrano pepper, coconut milk and tomatoes while cooking. Cover and lock the lid. Seal the pressure release valve,
3. Select the *Manual* function at low pressure for 5 minutes, When it beeps; do a *Natural* release to release all the steam.
4. Remove the lid and squeeze in lemon juice, Garnish with fresh cilantro leaves and serve.

Beans, Peppers and Shrimp Mix

Prep time: 15 minutes | Cook time: 24 minutes | Serves 4

½ pound (226 g) great northern
    beans; rinsed, soaked and
    drained
½ small green bell pepper; seeded
    and chopped.
½ celery stalk; chopped.
1 ½ tablespoon olive oil
1 medium onion; chopped
1 garlic clove; minced
1 tablespoon fresh parsley; chopped.
½ teaspoon red pepper flakes;
    crushed
½ teaspoon cayenne pepper
1 cup chicken broth
Water; as required
1 bay leaf
½ pound (226 g) medium shrimp; peeled and deveined

1. Select the *Sauté* function on your Instant pot then add the oil, onion, celery, bell pepper and cook for 5 minutes,
2. Now add the parsley, garlic, spices and bay leaf to the pot and cook for another 2 minutes,
3. Pour in the chicken broth then add beans to it. Secure the cooker lid. Select the *Manual* function for 15 minutes with medium pressure,
4. When it beeps; do a Natural release in 10 minutes and remove the lid. Add shrimp to the beans and cook them together on the *Manual* function for 2 minutes at high pressure,
5. Do a Quick release; keep it aside for 10 minutes then remove the lid. Serve hot.

Shrimp Pasta with Alfredo Tuscan Sauce

Prep time: 15 minutes | Cook time: 5 minutes | Serves 3

1 pound (454 g) shrimp
1 jar alfredo sauce
1 ½ cups fresh spinach
1 cup sun-dried tomatoes
1 box penne pasta
1 ½ teaspoon Tuscan seasoning
3 cups water

1. Add the water and pasta to a pot over a medium heat, boil until it cooks completely. Then strain the pasta and keep it aside.
2. Select the "Sauté" function on your Instant Pot and add the tomatoes, shrimp, Tuscan seasoning, and alfredo sauce into it.
3. Stir and cook until shrimp turn pink in color. Now add the spinach leaves to the pot and cook for 5 minutes.
4. Add the pasta to the pot and stir well. Serve hot.

Lobster Rolls with Mayonnais

Prep time: 10 minutes | Cook time: 4 minutes | Serves 2

¼ teaspoons celery salt

4 tablespoons melted butter

2 teaspoons old bay seasoning

3 scallions, chopped

½ cup mayonnaise

1 lemon, cut in half

1 ½ cups chicken broth

2 pounds (907 g) Maine Lobster Tails

2 hot dog buns (sliced in half)

1. Add the chicken broth and a teaspoon of old bay seasoning to the insert of the Instant Pot. Set the steamer trivet inside it.
2. Place the lobster tails with their meat sides up, over the trivet.
3. Cook the lobster tails on the "Manual" function on high pressure for 4 minutes.
4. Meanwhile, prepare an ice bath for the tails. After the beep, do a quick release then remove the lid.
5. Transfer the lobster tails immediately to the ice bath and let them rest.
6. Use kitchen shears to cut the underbelly of each tail and remove the meat from it. Dice down the meat into edible chunks.
7. Add all the remaining ingredients, except the hot dog buns, into a bowl and whisk them well.
8. Add the lobster to the mixture, mix them then refrigerate it for 15 minutes.
9. Prepare the buns by heating them in a skillet greased with melted butter.
10. Use the refrigerated lobster mix to fill the buns. Serve.

Seafood Platter

Prep time: 10 minutes | Cook time: 40 minutes | Serves 4

½ pound (226 g) medium-sized red potatoes, halved

1 cup seafood stock

1 ½ tablespoons Cajun's shrimp boil

½ pound (226 g) clams, fresh frozen

½ pound (226 g) shell on shrimp, deveined

½ pound (226 g) mussels, fresh or frozen

1 lemon, quartered

½ pound (226 g) smoked Kielbasa, cut into 2-inch pieces

1 tablespoon chopped parsley

Cilantro and lemon wedges (Garnish)

1. Add the seafood stock, boiling spice, and potatoes to the Instant Pot.
2. Cover the lid and let it "Slow Cook" for 30 minutes till the potatoes get tender.
3. Remove the lid and add the clams, shrimp, mussels, Kielbasa, and lemon to the pot.
4. Cook for 10 minutes if you are using frozen seafood, else cook for only 5 minutes.
5. Garnish with cilantro and lemon wedges on top. Serve.

Chapter 10 Vegetables

Bell Peppers, Pine Nuts, and Onion

Prep time: 5 minutes | Cook time: 15 minutes | Serves 4

1 pound (454 g) mixed bell peppers, cut into wedges
1 cup veggie stock
¼ cup pine nuts, toasted
1 tablespoon olive oil
1 tablespoon spring onions, chopped

1. In your instant pot, combine the bell peppers with the rest of the ingredients, put the lid on and cook on High for 15 minutes.
2. Release the pressure naturally for 10 minutes, divide the mix between plates and serve.

Garlicky Brussels Sprouts

Prep time: 5 minutes | Cook time: 20 minutes | Serves 4

1 pound (454 g) Brussels sprouts
1 cup chicken stock
2 green onions, chopped
4 garlic cloves, minced
A pinch of salt and black pepper
1 tablespoon dill, chopped

1. In your instant pot, mix the sprouts with the stock and the rest of the ingredients, put the lid on and cook on High for 20 minutes.
2. Release the pressure naturally for 10 minutes, divide the mix between plates and serve.

Balsamic Green Beans and Beets

Prep time: 10 minutes | Cook time: 20 minutes | Serves 4

1½ cups chicken stock
4 beets, peeled and cubed
1 red onion, sliced
1 pound (454 g) green beans, trimmed and halved
A pinch of salt and black pepper
1 tablespoon dill, chopped
1 tablespoon balsamic vinegar

1. In your instant pot, combine the beets with the green beans and the rest of the ingredients, put the lid on and cook on High for 20 minutes.
2. Release the pressure naturally for 10 minutes, divide everything between plates and serve.

Hot Zucchinis

Prep time: 5 minutes | Cook time: 10 minutes | Serves 4

4 zucchinis, roughly cubed
¼ cup chicken stock
1 tablespoon chili powder
½ teaspoon cayenne pepper
½ teaspoon red pepper flakes

1. In your instant pot, mix the zucchinis with the rest of the ingredients, put the lid on and cook on High for 10 minutes.
2. Release the pressure naturally for 10 minutes, divide the mix between plates and serve.

Herb Sweet Potatoes

Prep time: 10 minutes | Cook time: 8 minutes | Serves 4

2 pounds (907 g) sweet potatoes, peeled and cut into 1-inch chunks
1 teaspoon minced fresh thyme
½ teaspoon minced fresh rosemary
1 tablespoon extra-virgin olive oil (optional)
½ teaspoon fine sea salt
Freshly ground black pepper, to taste

1. Pour 1 cup water into the Instant Pot and arrange a steamer basket on the bottom. Place the sweet potatoes in the basket, making sure the potatoes don't touch the water. Secure the lid and move the steam release valve to Sealing. Select Manual/Pressure Cook to cook on high pressure for 8 minutes.
2. When the cooking cycle is complete, quickly release the pressure by moving the steam release valve to Venting. When the floating valve drops, remove the lid and press Cancel to stop the cooking cycle. Use oven mitts to lift out the steam basket and pour the water out of the pot.
3. Pour the drained sweet potatoes back into the pot and use a potato masher to mash the potatoes. Add the thyme, rosemary, olive oil, salt, and several grinds of pepper and stir well to combine. Taste and adjust the seasonings, then serve warm. Store leftovers in an airtight container in the fridge for 5 days.

Vegetable Medley

Prep time: 5 minutes | Cook time: 1 minute | Serves 4

1 pound (454 g) assorted non-starchy vegetables, such as cauliflower, carrots, and green beans
2 tablespoons extra-virgin olive oil
1 clove garlic, minced
Fine sea salt and freshly ground black pepper, to taste
Chopped fresh parsley, for garnish

1. Pour 1 cup water into the Instant Pot and arrange a steamer basket on the bottom. Place the vegetables in the steamer basket, making sure the vegetables aren't touching the water. Secure the lid and move the steam release valve to Sealing. Select Manual/Pressure Cook to cook on high pressure for 0 minutes.
2. When the pot beeps and the screen reads L0:00, immediately move the steam release valve to Venting to quickly release the steam pressure. When the floating valve drops, remove the lid and press Cancel to stop the cooking cycle. The vegetables should be tender, but with some tooth to them. Use oven mitts to remove the steamer basket full of vegetables, drain the water from the pot, then dry the pot and return it to the Instant Pot housing.
3. Press Sauté and add the olive oil to the Instant Pot. Once the oil is hot but not smoking, add in the garlic and stir briefly, just until fragrant, about 30 seconds. Add the steamed vegetables to the pot and stir well to coat them in the garlic-infused olive oil, about 30 seconds more.
4. Season generously with salt and pepper, then serve warm with parsley on top. Store leftover vegetables in an airtight container in the fridge for 1 week. They make for great toppings in a salad or grain bowl.

Spicy Green Beans

Prep time: 10 minutes | Cook time: 1 minute | Serves 4

1 pound (454 g) green beans, trimmed and cut into 1-inch pieces
1 tablespoon extra-virgin olive oil
2 cloves garlic, minced
1½ teaspoons toasted sesame oil
¼ teaspoon red pepper flakes
Fine sea salt, to taste
1 tablespoon sesame seeds

1. Pour 1 cup water into the Instant Pot and arrange a steamer basket on the bottom. Add the green beans to the basket, making sure the beans don't touch the water. Secure the lid and move the steam release valve to Sealing. Select Manual/Pressure Cook and cook at high pressure for 0 minutes.
2. When the pot beeps and the screen reads L0:00, quickly release the pressure by moving the steam release valve to Venting. When the floating valve drops, remove the lid and press Cancel to stop the cooking cycle. Use oven mitts to remove the steamer basket full of beans and set them aside. Drain the water from the pot.
3. Press Sauté and add the olive oil to the Instant Pot. Once the oil is hot but not smoking, add the garlic, sesame oil, and red pepper flakes. Stir briefly, about 30 seconds, then add the steamed green beans and stir well to coat the beans in the fragrant oil, about 30 seconds more.
4. Season with salt to taste (I use ½ teaspoon), and serve warm with a sprinkling of sesame seeds on top. Store leftovers in an airtight container in the fridge for 5 days; they make a great chilled topping for salads.

Bacon, Potato, Jalapeño Frittata

Prep time: 10 minutes | Cook time: 25 minutes | Serves 4

1½ pounds (680 g) small red or gold
    potatoes
8 large eggs
½ cup thinly sliced green onions,
    plus more for serving
4 slices Whole30-compliant bacon,
    crisp-cooked and crumbled
¼ cup Whole30-compliant pickled
    jalapeños, chopped
¼ cup chopped fresh parsley
½ teaspoon salt
½ teaspoon black pepper
Clarified butter or ghee, for greasing
½ teaspoon paprika
Whole30-compliant salsa
Whole30 Sriracha or Whole30-compliant hot sauce (optional)

1. Place the potatoes in a 6-quart Instant Pot. Add ½ cup water. Lock the lid in place.
2. Select Manual and cook on high pressure for 5 minutes. Use natural release. Discard water. Let the potatoes cool until easy to handle.
3. Meanwhile, combine the eggs, green onions, bacon, pickled jalapeños, parsley, salt, and black pepper. Slice the potatoes. Carefully stir into the egg mixture.
4. Place the rack in the pot. Add 1½ cups water. Grease a 1-quart soufflé dish with butter or ghee. Pour the egg mixture into the prepared dish. Sprinkle with the paprika. Place the dish on the rack. Lock the lid in place.
5. Select Manual and cook on high pressure for 20 minutes. Use natural release. Carefully remove the dish. Let the frittata cool on a wire rack for at least 10 minutes before slicing.
6. Spoon salsa on servings, top with additional sliced green onions, and serve with sriracha or hot sauce if desired.

Brazilian Rosemary Potato Curry

Prep time: 10 minutes | Cook time: 30 minutes | Serves 2

1 large potato; peeled and diced
½ tablespoons rosemary
½ tablespoons cayenne pepper
1 small onion; peeled and diced
8 ounces (227 g) fresh tomatoes
1 tablespoon olive oil
2 tablespoons garlic cloves grated
1½ tablespoons thyme
Salt and pepper, to taste

1. Pour a cup of water into the instant pot and place the steamer trivet inside,
2. Place the potatoes and half the garlic over the trivet and sprinkle some salt and pepper on top.
3. Secure the lid and cook on Steam function for 20 minutes,
4. After it beeps Natural Release the steam and remove the lid.
5. Put the potatoes to one side and empty the pot.
6. Add the remaining Ingredients to the cooker and Sauté for 10 minutes,
7. Use an immerse blender to puree the cooked mixture, Stir in the steamed potatoes and serve hot.

Green Beans with Bacon

Prep time: 10 minutes | Cook time: 8 minutes | Serves 6

2 (6-ounce / 170-g) packages
    Whole30-compliant Canadian
    bacon, chopped
½ cup scallions, chopped
2 cloves garlic, minced
1 pound (454 g) green beans,
    trimmed
Kosher salt and ground black
    pepper, to taste
½ teaspoon paprika
½ teaspoon dried dill weed
½ teaspoon red pepper flakes
2 tablespoons apple cider vinegar
1 cup water

1. Press the "Sauté" button to heat up your Instant Pot. Once hot, cook Canadian bacon until crisp, about 4 minutes; reserve.
2. Add the scallions and garlic. Cook an additional 1 minute or until aromatic.
3. Add the other ingredients; stir to combine
4. Secure the lid. Choose "Manual" mode and Low pressure; cook for 3 minutes. Once cooking is complete, use a quick pressure release; carefully remove the lid.
5. Serve warm, garnished with the reserved bacon. Bon appétit!

Vegetable Medley with Sausage

Prep time: 10 minutes | Cook time: 10 minutes | Serves 4

2 tablespoons olive oil

2 garlic cloves, minced

½ cup scallions

2 pork sausages, casing removed, sliced

2 cups cauliflower, chopped into small florets

½ pound (227 g) button mushrooms, sliced

2 bell peppers, chopped

1 red chili pepper, chopped

2 cups turnip greens

Sea salt and freshly ground black pepper, to taste

1 teaspoon cayenne pepper

2 bay leaves

1 cup water

1. Press the "Sauté" button to heat up your Instant Pot. Heat the oil and sauté the garlic and scallions until aromatic, about 2 minutes.
2. Add sausage and cook an additional 3 minutes or until it is no longer pink. Now, stir in the remaining ingredients.
3. Secure the lid. Choose "Manual" mode and High pressure; cook for 5 minutes. Once cooking is complete, use a quick pressure release; carefully remove the lid. Bon appétit!

Satarash

Prep time: 15 minutes | Cook time: 5 minutes | Serves 4

2 tablespoons olive oil

1 white onion, chopped

2 cloves garlic

1 red bell pepper, seeded and sliced

1 green bell pepper, seeded and sliced

2 ripe tomatoes, puréed

½ teaspoon turmeric

1 teaspoon paprika

1/2 teaspoon dried oregano

Kosher salt and ground black pepper, to taste

1 cup water

4 large eggs, lightly whisked

1. Press the "Sauté" button to heat up your Instant Pot. Heat the oil and sauté the onion and garlic until aromatic, about 2 minutes.
2. Add the peppers, tomatoes, turmeric, paprika, oregano, salt, black pepper, and water.
3. Secure the lid. Choose "Manual" mode and High pressure; cook for 3 minutes. Once cooking is complete, use a quick pressure release; carefully remove the lid.
4. Fold in the eggs and stir to combine. Cover with the lid and let it sit in the residual heat for 5 minutes. Serve warm.

Whole Cauliflower in Tomato-Meat Sauce

Prep time: 15 minutes | Cook time: 20 minutes | Serves 4

1 pound (454 g) ground lamb or beef

1 medium yellow onion, chopped

3 cloves garlic, minced

2 teaspoons ancho chile powder

1 teaspoon dried oregano, crushed

½ teaspoon salt

1 stick (3 inches) cinnamon

1 bay leaf

¼ cup Whole30-compliant tomato paste

1 can (14½-ounce / 411.1-g) Whole30-compliant beef broth

1 can (14½-ounce / 411.1-g) Whole30-compliant diced tomatoes, undrained

1 medium head cauliflower

¼ cup chopped fresh parsley

1. On a 6-quart Instant Pot, select Sauté and adjust to Normal/Medium. Add the lamb and onion. Cook, stirring occasionally with a wooden spoon to break up the meat, until browned, 8 to 10 minutes. Add the garlic, chile powder, oregano, salt, cinnamon stick, and bay leaf. Cook for 1 minute. Add the tomato paste and cook for 1 minute. Stir in the broth and tomatoes. Remove the leaves from the cauliflower. Trim the stem so the cauliflower stands upright. Add the cauliflower, stem side down, to the pot. Lock the lid in place.
2. Select Manual and cook on high pressure for 10 minutes. Use quick release.
3. Carefully remove the cauliflower from the pot. Cut into 4 wedges. Discard the cinnamon stick and bay leaf. Stir the parsley into the sauce. Serve the sauce with the cauliflower.

Balsamic Dill Cauliflower

Prep time: 10 minutes | Cook time: 12 minutes | Serves 4

1 pound (454 g) cauliflower florets
2 garlic cloves, minced
1 cup chicken stock
A pinch of salt and black pepper
1 cup tomato sauce
1 tablespoon balsamic vinegar
1 tablespoon dill, chopped

1. In your instant pot, mix the cauliflower with the rest of the ingredients except the dill, put the lid on and cook on High for 12 minutes.
2. Release the pressure naturally for 10 minutes, divide the cauliflower between plates, sprinkle the dill on top and serve.

Garlicky Celeriac

Prep time: 5 minutes | Cook time: 15 minutes | Serves 4

1 celeriac, cut into sticks
1 tablespoon avocado oil
4 garlic cloves, minced
1 cup chicken stock
A pinch of salt and black pepper
1 tablespoon dill, chopped

1. Set your instant pot on Sauté mode, add the oil, heat it up, add the garlic and brown for 2 minutes.
2. Add the celeriac and the rest of the ingredients, put the lid on and cook on High for 13 minutes more.
3. Release the pressure naturally for 10 minutes, divide the mix between plates and serve.

Green Beans with Bacon and Walnuts

Prep time: 5 minutes | Cook time: 8 minutes | Serves 4

5 strips Whole30-compliant raw
    bacon, chopped
1 tablespoon (14 g) ghee or clarified
    butter
¼ cup (60 ml) low-sodium chicken
    stock
12 ounces (340 g) washed and
    trimmed green beans
Salt and freshly ground black
    pepper, to taste
2 ounces (57 g) walnuts

1. Press sauté on the Instant Pot. Add the chopped bacon. Cook for 5 to 6 minutes, or until crispy. Remove the crisp bacon with a slotted spoon and transfer to a paper towel–lined plate.
2. Press cancel. Stir the butter and stock into the bacon fat. Use a wooden spoon to scrape up any browned bacon bits from the bottom of the pot.
3. Add the green beans to the pot. Season with salt and pepper to taste. Toss to evenly coat the beans.
4. Secure the lid with the steam vent in the sealed position. Press steam. Use the plus and minus buttons to adjust the time until the display reads "1 minute."
5. While the beans steam, heat a small, dry skillet over medium heat. Add the walnuts and toast them for 2 minutes. Remove from the heat and chop.
6. When the timer sounds, quick release the pressure. Remove the lid and toss the beans with tongs.
7. Transfer the beans and sauce to a plate. Top with the bacon and walnuts.

Bell Peppers with Cilantro

Prep time: 5 minutes | Cook time: 15 minutes | Serves 4

1 pound (454 g) mixed bell peppers,
    cut into thick strips
½ cup veggie stock
3 garlic cloves, minced
A pinch of cayenne pepper
A pinch of salt and black pepper
1 tablespoon cilantro, chopped

1. In your instant pot, combine the bell peppers with the stock and the rest of the ingredients, put the lid on and cook on High for 15 minutes.
2. Release the pressure naturally for 10 minutes, divide the mix between plates and serve.

Balsamic Collard Greens with Tomato

Prep time: 5 minutes | Cook time: 20 minutes | Serves 4

1 bunch collard greens, trimmed
½ cup chicken stock
2 tablespoons tomato puree
A pinch of salt and black pepper
1 tablespoon balsamic vinegar

1. In your instant pot, mix the collard greens with the stock and the rest of the ingredients, put the lid on and cook on High for 20 minutes.
2. Release the pressure naturally for 10 minutes, divide the mix between plates and serve.

Green Beans, Bacon, and Mushrooms

Prep time: 10 minutes | Cook time: 8 minutes | Serves 4

1 pound (454 g) fresh green beans, trimmed
Water as needed
6 ounces (170 g) Whole30-compliant bacon, chopped
1 clove garlic, minced
1 small yellow onion, chopped
8 ounces (227 g) mushrooms, sliced
Salt and ground black pepper, to taste
A splash of balsamic vinegar

1. Add the beans to the Instant Pot. Add water to cover the beans.
2. Close and secure the lid. Select MANUAL and cook at HIGH pressure for 3 minutes.
3. Once cooking is complete, select Cancel and let Naturally Release for 10 minutes.
4. Unlock the pot. Drain the beans and leave them aside for now.
5. Select the SAUTÉ setting on the Instant Pot. Add the bacon and sauté for 1 or 2 minutes stirring often.
6. Add the garlic and onion, stir and cook for 2 minutes
7. Add the mushrooms, stir and cook until they are soft
8. Add cooked beans, salt, pepper and a splash of vinegar, stir well.
9. Press the CANCEL button to stop the cooking program. Serve.

Celery in Tomato Sauce

Prep time: 5 minutes | Cook time: 15 minutes | Serves 4

4 celery stalks, roughly chopped
A pinch of salt and black pepper
1 tablespoon tomato sauce
½ cup chicken stock
1 tablespoon parsley, chopped

1. In your instant pot, mix the celery with the rest of the ingredients, put the lid on and cook on High for 15 minutes.
2. Release the pressure naturally for 10 minutes, divide the mix between plates and serve.

Paprika Dill Okra Mix

Prep time: 5 minutes | Cook time: 10 minutes | Serves 4

2 cups okra
A pinch of salt and black pepper
1 cup tomato sauce
1 tablespoon sweet paprika
2 tablespoon dill, chopped

1. In your instant pot, mix the okra with salt, pepper and the rest of the ingredients, put the lid on and cook on High for 10 minutes.
2. Release the pressure naturally for 10 minutes, divide the mix between plates and serve.

Dijon Artichokes

Prep time: 10 minutes | Cook time: 12 minutes | Serves 4

4 medium to large globe artichokes
Juice of 1 lemon, divided
1 cup water
1 teaspoon Dijon mustard
1 clove garlic
¼ teaspoon sea salt, plus more to taste
4 tablespoons ghee, melted

1. Prepare your artichokes. Remove the outer leaves, trim about ½ inch from the top and remove the stem so each artichoke can sit upright. Brush each artichoke with lemon juice, reserve the remaining lemon juice and set aside.
2. Pour the water into the Instant Pot and insert the steam trivet. Arrange the artichokes, stem side down, on the trivet so they sit upright.
3. Secure the lid with the steam vent in the sealed position. Select manual or pressure, and cook on high pressure for 12 to 15 minutes (12 for medium artichokes, 15 for large ones). Use a quick release.
4. Meanwhile, prepare the lemon-garlic butter. In a small bowl, stir the Dijon, remaining lemon juice, garlic and salt into the butter.
5. Serve warm with the lemon-garlic butter on the side for dipping. Sprinkle with additional salt to taste.

Butternut and Root Vegetables with Herb

Prep time: 15 minutes | Cook time: 11 minutes | Serves 4

2 tablespoons ghee or clarified butter
2 cloves garlic, minced
1 cup cubed butternut squash (1" cubes)
1 cup sliced carrot
1 cup cubed turnip (1" cubes)
1 large fennel bulb, cut into ½" pieces
¼ teaspoon baking soda
1 tablespoon herbes de Provence
½ teaspoon sea salt, plus more to taste
¾ cup chicken or vegetable stock
1 tablespoon fresh rosemary, for garnish
1 tablespoon fresh thyme, for garnish

1. Select sauté on the Instant Pot. Once hot, add the butter and garlic. Cook for about 1 minute, then add the butternut squash. Cook for another 4 to 5 minutes, or until the squash is lightly browned. Select cancel.
2. Add the carrot, turnip and fennel. Sprinkle the vegetables with the baking soda, herbes de Provence and salt. Pour the stock on top of the vegetable mixture.
3. Secure the lid with the steam vent in the sealed position. Select manual, and cook on high pressure for 6 minutes.
4. Use a quick release, and ensure all the steam is released before removing the lid.
5. Serve warm, garnished with the rosemary, thyme and additional salt to taste.

Brussels Sprouts with Bacon

Prep time: 10 minutes | Cook time: 8 minutes | Serves 8 to 10

1 cup water
2 pounds (907 g) Brussels sprouts, trimmed and halved
4 tablespoons ghee or avocado oil
3 cloves garlic, minced
1 teaspoon finely chopped fresh thyme leaves
1 teaspoon sea salt
4 ounces (113 g) Whole30-compliant precooked crispy bacon or turkey bacon, crumbled

1. Place the water in the Instant Pot and insert a steamer basket. Layer the Brussels sprouts in the steamer basket.
2. Secure the lid with the steam vent in the sealed position. Press manual and set on high pressure for 2 minutes.
3. Once the timer sounds, press keep warm/cancel. Allow the Instant Pot to release pressure naturally for 10 minutes. Using an oven mitt, do a quick release. If there is any steam left over, allow it to release until the silver dial drops, then carefully open the lid.
4. Carefully remove the Brussels sprouts and steamer basket, setting the Brussels sprouts aside. Pour out and discard the water that remains in the pot.
5. Place your healthy fat of choice in the Instant Pot and press sauté. Once the fat has melted, add the garlic and thyme and sauté for 1 minute, stirring occasionally. Add the Brussels sprouts back to the pot along with the salt and sauté until they start to turn golden brown, about 4 minutes. Add the crumbled bacon and give everything a stir, then sauté for 1 minute to warm the bacon. Press keep warm/cancel.
6. Serve immediately.

Lush Summer Ratatouille

Prep time: 15 minutes | Cook time: 11 minutes | Serves 6

⅓ cup avocado oil or olive oil, divided

1 large white onion, diced

⅓ cup fresh lemon juice

3 cloves garlic, minced

2 tablespoons tomato paste

1 cup loosely packed fresh basil, plus more for garnish

2 tablespoons white wine vinegar

1 teaspoon sea salt, plus more to taste

1 small eggplant, diced

2 medium zucchini, diced

2 medium yellow summer squash, diced

1 pound (454 g) cherry or grape tomatoes

1. Select sauté on the Instant Pot, set to "medium," if possible. Coat the bottom of the pot with 2 tablespoons (30 ml) of the oil, then add the onion. Sauté for 3 minutes, or until translucent and fragrant. Select cancel.
2. Meanwhile, prepare the lemon-basil sauce: In a food processor, combine the remaining oil, lemon juice, garlic, tomato paste, basil, vinegar and salt. Pulse until smooth.
3. Place the eggplant, zucchini, squash and tomatoes in the Instant Pot. Pour the lemon-basil sauce over the vegetable mixture.
4. Secure the lid with the steam vent in the sealed position. Select manual or pressure, and cook on high pressure for 8 minutes.
5. Use a natural release.
6. Serve hot with more basil for garnish, and additional salt to taste.

Dried Herb Carrots and Parsnips

Prep time: 10 minutes | Cook time: 7 minutes | Serves 4 to 6

1 cup water

4 large carrots, peeled and thickly sliced on the diagonal

3 medium parsnips, peeled and sliced on the diagonal

3 tablespoons ghee

2 cloves garlic, minced

1 teaspoon sea salt

1 teaspoon dried thyme

1 teaspoon dried dill

1. Pour the water into the Instant Pot and insert a steamer basket. Layer the carrots and parsnips in the steamer basket.
2. Secure the lid with the steam vent in the sealed position. Press manual and set on high pressure for 3 minutes.
3. Once the timer sounds, press keep warm/cancel. Using an oven mitt, do a quick release. When the steam venting stops and the silver dial drops, carefully open the lid.
4. Carefully remove the carrots and parsnips and steamer basket, setting the carrots and parsnips aside. Pour out and discard the water that remains in the pot.
5. Place your healthy fat of choice in the Instant Pot and press sauté. Once the fat has melted, add the garlic and sauté for 1 minute, stirring occasionally. Add the carrots and parsnips back to the pot along with the salt, thyme and dill. Give everything a stir, then sauté for 3 minutes, stirring occasionally. Press keep warm/cancel.
6. Serve immediately.

Lemon-Garlic Smashed Red Potatoes

Prep time: 10 minutes | Cook time: 10 minutes | Serves 4

1½ pounds (680 g) baby red potatoes

1 cup water

2 tablespoons avocado oil or extra-virgin olive oil

3 cloves garlic, minced

½ teaspoon sea salt, plus more to taste

½ teaspoon freshly ground black pepper

2 tablespoons fresh lemon juice

1. Turn on the oven to broil.
2. Wash and dry the potatoes. Pour the water into the Instant Pot and insert the steam trivet. Place the potatoes on the trivet.
3. Secure the lid with the steam vent in the sealed position. Select manual or pressure, and cook on high pressure for 6 minutes.
4. Use a quick release. Remove the potatoes and place on a large baking sheet. Using a glass or the back of a spoon, gently press down on the potatoes, or smash them.
5. In a small bowl, whisk together the oil and garlic. Brush over each of the potatoes, then sprinkle with salt and pepper.
6. Transfer the potatoes to the oven. Broil for 4 to 5 minutes, or until crispy.
7. Remove from the oven and drizzle with the lemon juice. Sprinkle with additional salt to taste. Serve hot.

Asian-Flavor Baby Bok Choy

Prep time: 10 minutes | Cook time: 5 minutes | Serves 4

3 tablespoons ghee
1 (¾-inch) piece fresh ginger, peeled and finely minced
3 cloves garlic, minced
¾ teaspoon sea salt
3 tablespoons coconut aminos
½ cup filtered water
7 baby bok choy, cut in half down the middle
1 scallion, white and light green parts only, sliced on a bias
1 teaspoon toasted sesame oil, for garnish

1. Place your healthy fat of choice in the Instant Pot and press sauté. Once the fat has melted, add the ginger and garlic and sauté for 2 minutes, stirring occasionally. Press keep warm/cancel.
2. Add the salt, coconut aminos and water, then add the bok choy and scallion and give the mixture a gentle stir.
3. Secure the lid with the steam vent in the sealed position. Press manual and set on high pressure for 3 minutes.
4. Once the timer sounds, press keep warm/cancel. Allow the Instant Pot to release pressure naturally for 5 minutes. Using an oven mitt, do a quick release. If there is any steam left over, allow it to release until the silver dial drops, then carefully open the lid.
5. Serve immediately, drizzled with the toasted sesame oil.

Tomatoes and Green Beans

Prep time: 5 minutes | Cook time: 7 minutes | Serves 4 to 6

1 teaspoon olive oil
1 clove garlic, crushed
2 cups fresh, chopped tomatoes
½ cup water
1 pound (454 g) trimmed green beans
Salt, to taste

1. Select the SAUTÉ setting on the Instant Pot and heat the oil.
2. Add the garlic and sauté until fragrant and golden. Add tomatoes and stir. If the tomatoes are dry, add ½ cup water.
3. Put the green beans in the Instant Pot and sprinkle with salt.
4. Close and secure the lid. Select MANUAL and cook at HIGH pressure for 5 minutes.
5. Once pressure cooking is complete, use a Quick Release.
6. If the beans aren't quite tender enough, sauté in sauce for a few minutes. Serve.

Fresh Herb-Orange Blistered Olives

Prep time: 10 minutes | Cook time: 6 minutes | Serves 16

1 cup water
1 pound (454 g) any variety green olives
1 pound (454 g) any variety marinated black olives (not canned black olives)
2 lemons, sliced
1 orange, sliced
3 tablespoons ghee or avocado oil
4 cloves garlic, minced
2 teaspoons fresh thyme leaves
1 teaspoon fresh rosemary leaves, finely chopped

1. Pour the water into the Instant Pot and insert the steamer basket. Layer the olives and citrus slices in the steamer basket.
2. Secure the lid with the steam vent in the sealed position. Press manual and set on high pressure for 1 minute.
3. Once the timer sounds, press keep warm/cancel. Using an oven mitt, do a quick release. When the steam venting stops and the silver dial drops, carefully open the lid.
4. Carefully remove the olives, citrus slices and steamer basket, setting the olives and citrus slices aside. Pour out and discard the water that remains in the pot.
5. Place your healthy fat of choice in the Instant Pot and press sauté. Once the fat has melted, add the garlic and sauté for 2 minutes, stirring occasionally. Add the olives and citrus slices back to the pot along with the thyme, and rosemary. Give everything a stir, then sauté for 3 minutes, stirring occasionally. Press keep warm/cancel.
6. Serve immediately.

Green Beans with Bacon

Prep time: 5 minutes | Cook time: 15 minutes | Serves 4 to 6

1 cup water

1½ pounds (680 g) green beans, ends trimmed

3 tablespoons ghee

4 cloves garlic, minced

1 teaspoon sea salt

4 ounces (113 g) Whole30-compliant precooked crispy bacon or turkey bacon, crumbled

1. Pour the water into the Instant Pot and insert a steamer basket. Layer the green beans in the steamer basket.
2. Secure the lid with the steam vent in the sealed position. Press manual and set on high pressure for 2 minutes.
3. Once the timer sounds, press keep warm/cancel. Allow the Instant Pot to release pressure naturally for 10 minutes. Using an oven mitt, do a quick release. If there is any steam left over, allow it to release until the silver dial drops, then carefully open the lid.
4. Carefully remove the green beans and steamer basket, setting the green beans aside. Pour out and discard the water that remains in the pot.
5. Place your healthy fat of choice in the Instant Pot and press sauté. Once the fat has melted, add the garlic and sauté for 2 minutes, stirring occasionally. Add the green beans back to the pot along with the salt and crumbled bacon. Give everything a stir, then sauté for 1 minute to warm the bacon. Press keep warm/cancel.
6. Serve immediately.

Steamed Green Beans with Vinegar Dressing

Prep time: 10 minutes | Cook time: 1 minutes | Serves 2 to 4

1 cup water

1 pound (454 g) green beans, washed

2 tablespoons fresh parsley, chopped, for garnish

For the Dressing:

3 tablespoons olive oil

2 tablespoons white wine vinegar

3 cloves garlic, sliced

1 pinch of ground black pepper

1 pinch of salt

1. Pour the water into the Instant Pot and insert a steamer basket. Put the green beans in the basket.
2. Close and secure the lid. Select the MANUAL setting and set the cooking time for 1 minute at HIGH pressure.
3. When the timer goes off, use a Quick Release. Carefully open the lid.
4. Transfer the beans into a serving bowl.
5. Stir in the dressing ingredients and let stand for 10 minutes.
6. Remove the slices of garlic, then garnish with the parsley. Serve.

Orange Beets

Prep time: 5 minutes | Cook time: 22 minutes | Serves 4 to 6

1 cup water

5 medium beets, about 2" in diameter, leaves removed

2 tablespoons grass-fed butter, ghee or avocado oil

¾ teaspoon sea salt

Zest of 1 orange

Juice of 1 orange

1. Pour the water into the Instant Pot and insert a steamer basket. Place the beets in the steamer basket.
2. Secure the lid with the steam vent in the sealed position. Press manual and set on high pressure for 20 minutes.
3. Once the timer sounds, press keep warm/cancel. Allow the Instant Pot to release pressure naturally for 15 minutes. Using an oven mitt, do a quick release. If there is any steam left over, allow it to release until the silver dial drops, then carefully open the lid.
4. Carefully remove the beets and steamer basket, setting the beets aside on a cutting board or large plate. Pour out and discard the water that remains in the pot.
5. Slice off the tops of the beets and carefully slide or cut off the skin—it should come off very easily— then discard the tops and peeled-off skin. Using a sharp knife, slice the beets into round slices about ¼ inch (6 mm) thick.
6. Place your healthy fat of choice in the Instant Pot and press sauté. Once the fat has melted, add the beets back to the pot along with the salt and the orange zest and juice, gently stirring occasionally for 2 minutes to warm the citrus. Press keep warm/cancel.
7. Serve immediately.

Vegetable Dish

1 tablespoon extra virgin olive oil
1 red onion, sliced
2 red bell peppers, sliced thinly
2 green bell pepper, sliced thinly
1 yellow bell peppers, sliced thinly
2 tomatoes, chopped
Salt and ground black pepper to taste
2 cloves garlic, chopped
1 bunch parsley, finely chopped

1. Select the SAUTÉ setting on the Instant Pot and heat the oil.
2. Add the onion and sauté for 3 minutes.
3. Add the bell peppers, stir and sauté for another 5 minutes.
4. Add the tomatoes and sprinkle with salt and pepper. Mix well. Close and lock the lid.
5. Press the CANCEL button to reset the cooking program, then press the MANUAL button and set the cooking time for 6 minutes at HIGH pressure.
6. Once pressure cooking is complete, select CANCEL and use a Quick Release. Carefully unlock the lid.
7. Transfer the veggies to a serving bowl and add the garlic and parsley. Stir well.
8. Serve.

Cauliflower Curry

Prep time: 5 minutes | Cook time: 4 minutes | Serves 2 to 4

16 ounces (453 g) cauliflower florets
1 can full-fat coconut milk
6 teaspoon garam masala
2 cups water
Salt and ground black pepper to taste

1. In the Instant Pot, combine the cauliflower, coconut milk, garam masala, and water.
2. Season with salt and pepper, stir well.
3. Close and lock the lid. Select MANUAL and cook at HIGH pressure for 4 minutes.
4. When the timer goes off, use a Quick Release. Carefully open the lid.
5. Serve.

Steamed Artichokes

Prep time: 5 minutes | Cook time: 20 minutes | Serves 2 to 4

2 medium whole artichokes (about 6 ounces/ 170 g each)
1 lemon wedge
1 cup water

1. Wash the artichokes and remove any damaged outer leaves.
2. Trim off the stem and top edge. Rub the top with lemon wedge.
3. Prepare the Instant Pot by adding the water to the pot and placing the steamer basket in it.
4. Close and lock the lid. Select MANUAL and cook at HIGH pressure for 20 minutes.
5. Once cooking is complete, let the pressure Release Naturally for 10 minutes. Release any remaining steam manually. Uncover the pot.
6. Transfer the artichokes to a serving plate and serve warm with your favorite sauce.

Steamed Asparagus

Prep time: 5 minutes | Cook time: 2 minutes | Serves 2 to 4

1 pound (454 g) asparagus
1 cup water
4 teaspoon olive oil
1 tablespoon onion, chopped
Salt and fresh ground pepper to taste

1. Wash asparagus and trim off bottom of stems by about 1½ inches.
2. Prepare the Instant Pot by adding the water to the pot and placing the steam rack in it.
3. Place the asparagus on the steam rack. Brush the asparagus with the olive oil.
4. Sprinkle with the onion. Close and secure the lid.
5. Select the STEAM setting and set the cooking time for 2 minutes.
6. Once timer goes off, use a Quick Release. Carefully unlock the lid.
7. Season with salt and pepper and serve.

Spiced Carrots

Prep time: 10 minutes | Cook time: 25 minutes | Serves 4

2 and ½ pounds (1.133 kg) carrots, sliced
3 tablespoons avocado oil
Salt and black pepper to the taste
1 cup veggie stock
1 teaspoon garam masala
½ teaspoon sweet chili powder
1 teaspoon rosemary, dried

1. Set your instant pot on Sauté mode, add the oil, heat it up, add the carrots and brown for 5 minutes.
2. Add the rest of the ingredients, put the lid on and cook on High for 10 minutes.
3. Release the pressure naturally for 10 minutes, divide the mix between plates and serve as a side dish.

Parsnips and Beets Mix

Prep time: 10 minutes | Cook time: 20 minutes | Serves 4

1 pound (454 g) parsnips, peeled and roughly cubed
2 beets, peeled and roughly cubed
A pinch of salt and black pepper
1 cup veggie stock
½ teaspoon turmeric powder
1 tablespoon chives, chopped

1. In your instant pot, combine all the ingredients except the chives, put the lid on and cook on High for 10 minutes.
2. Release the pressure naturally for 10 minutes, divide the mix between plates and serve with the chives sprinkled on top.

Coconut Cauliflower Mash

Prep time: 10 minutes | Cook time: 8 minutes | Serves 4

1 pound (454 g) cauliflower florets
1 teaspoon Italian seasoning
1 teaspoon sage, dried
Salt and black pepper to the taste
2 spring onions, chopped
¼ cup coconut cream
½ cup chicken stock

1. In your instant pot, mix the cauliflower with the stock, salt, pepper, Italian seasoning and the sage, put the lid on and cook on High for 8 minutes.
2. Release the pressure naturally for 10 minutes, mash the mix with a potato masher, add the rest of the ingredients, whisk well, divide between plates and serve as a side dish.

Zucchini, Carrots and Eggplant Hash

Prep time: 10 minutes | Cook time: 15 minutes | Serves 4

½ cup veggie stock
1 zucchini, roughly cubed
1 eggplant, roughly cubed
2 carrots, sliced
2 tablespoons avocado oil
1 red onion, chopped
½ teaspoon oregano, dried
A pinch of salt and black pepper

1. Set the instant pot on Sauté mode, add the oil, heat it up, add the onion, salt, pepper and oregano, stir and cook for 3-4 minutes.
2. Add the rest of the ingredients, put the lid on and cook on High for 10 minutes.
3. Release the pressure fast for 5 minutes, divide the mix between plates and serve.

Chili Broccoli Sprouts

Prep time: 10 minutes | Cook time: 10 minutes | Serves 4

1 cup water
1 pound (454 g) broccoli sprouts
1 teaspoon sesame oil
1 teaspoon coconut aminos
1 teaspoon minced garlic
½ teaspoon chopped chili pepper
½ teaspoon salt

1. Pour the water into the Instant Pot. Lock the lid and bring the water to a boil on Sauté mode for about 10 minutes.
2. Open the lid and add the broccoli sprouts to the Instant Pot. Let sit in the hot water for 1 minute, then transfer to a bowl.
3. Whisk together the remaining ingredients in a separate bowl until combined.
4. Pour the mixture over the broccoli sprouts and gently toss to combine. Serve immediately.

Basil Tomato and Olive Stuffed Peppers

Prep time: 10 minutes | Cook time: 8 minutes | Serves 4

¼ cup tomato sauce
4 large bell peppers, trimmed
2 cup chopped tomatoes
Salt and pepper, to taste
4 basil leaves, chopped
½ cup chopped olives
1 cup water

1. Using a bowl, mix basil leaves, olives and tomatoes. Season with salt and pepper. Stuff bell peppers with the mixture.
2. Top with a drizzle of tomato sauce. In the Instant Pot, add the water. Add the steamer rack inside.
3. Carefully lay the bell peppers. Lock the lid. Set the Instant Pot to Pressure Cook mode, then set the timer for 8 minutes at High Pressure.
4. Once cooking is complete, do a quick pressure release. Carefully open the lid. Serve warm.

Rosemary Baby Potatoes

Prep time: 10 minutes | Cook time: 11 minutes | Serves 4

1 tablespoon olive oil
3 garlic cloves
2 pounds (907 g) baby potatoes
1 sprig rosemary
1 cup vegetable stock
Salt and pepper, to taste

1. Hit the Sauté button on the Instant Pot. Add the olive oil. Add the garlic, baby potatoes and rosemary.
2. Brown the outside of the potatoes. Pierce each potato with a fork. Add the vegetable stock.
3. Lock the lid. Set the Instant Pot to Pressure Cook mode, then set the timer for 11 minutes at High Pressure.
4. Once cooking is complete, do a quick pressure release. Carefully open the lid. Season with salt and pepper and serve.

Ritzy Veggie Medley

Prep time: 10 minutes | Cook time: 8 minutes | Serves 4

1 cup water
1 tablespoon raisins
1 zucchini, sliced
1 eggplant, cubed
3 tablespoons olive oil
10 halved cherry tomatoes
2 potatoes, cubed
2 tablespoons raisins

1. In the Instant Pot, add the water. Add the potatoes and zucchini. Lock the lid.
2. Set the Instant Pot to Pressure Cook mode, then set the timer for 8 minutes on High Pressure.
3. Once cooking is complete, do a quick pressure release. Carefully open the lid.
4. Drain water and add olive oil. Mix in the tomatoes and eggplant. Let cook for 2 minutes. Top with the raisins before serving.

Ratatouille

Prep time: 10 minutes | Cook time: 10 minutes | Serves 4

2 cups water
2 medium zucchini, sliced
3 tomatoes, sliced
2 eggplants, sliced
1 tablespoon olive oil
Salt and pepper, to taste

1. Pour the water into the Instant Pot. In a baking dish, arrange a layer of the zucchini.
2. Top with a layer of the tomatoes. Place a layer of eggplant slices on top. Continue layering until you use all the ingredients.
3. Drizzle with olive oil. Place the baking dish on the trivet and lower it. Lock the lid. Set the Instant Pot to Pressure Cook mode, then set the timer for 10 minutes at High Pressure.
4. Once cooking is complete, do a quick pressure release. Carefully open the lid. Sprinkle with salt and pepper and serve warm!

Coconut Potato Mash

Prep time: 5 minutes | Cook time: 8 minutes | Serves 4

2 tablespoons coconut oil
4 medium potatoes
1 teaspoon ground nutmeg
¼ cup coconut milk

1. Peel the potatoes and place them in the Instant Pot. Add enough water to cover them.
2. Lock the lid. Set the Instant Pot to Pressure Cook mode, then set the timer for 8 minutes at High Pressure.
3. Once cooking is complete, do a quick pressure release. Carefully open the lid. Drain any water present.
4. Mash the potatoes. Add the remaining ingredients. Serve immediately!

Buttery Thyme Cabbage

Prep time: 5 minutes | Cook time: 5 minutes | Serves 4

1 pound (454 g) white cabbage
2 tablespoons butter
1 teaspoon dried thyme
½ teaspoon salt
1 cup water

1. Cut the white cabbage on medium size petals and sprinkle with the butter, dried thyme and salt.
2. Place the cabbage petals in the Instant Pot pan.
3. Pour the water and insert the trivet in the Instant Pot. Put the pan on the trivet.
4. Set the lid in place. Select the Manual mode and set the cooking time for 5 minutes on High Pressure. When the timer goes off, do a quick pressure release. Carefully open the lid. Serve immediately.

Maple-Balsamic Parsnips

Prep time: 5 minutes | Cook time: 15 minutes | Serves 3

2 or 3 parsnips, peeled and cut into
　½-inch pieces
2 garlic cloves, minced
½ cup applesauce
¼ cup maple syrup
2 tablespoons balsamic vinegar
2 tablespoons extra-virgin olive oil
½ teaspoon dried thyme
¼ teaspoon sea salt

1. In the bowl of your Instant Pot, combine the parsnips, garlic, applesauce, maple syrup, vinegar, oil, thyme, and salt.
2. Secure the lid and seal the vent. Select Pressure Cook or Manual and cook on high pressure for 2 minutes, then quick release the pressure in the pot and remove the lid.
3. If the parsnips are too firm for your liking, cook for another minute on high pressure.

Delicious Brussels Sprouts with Potatoes

Prep time: 10 minutes | Cook time: 5 minutes | Serves 2 to 4

1½ pounds (680 g) Brussels sprouts
1 cup new potatoes cut into 1 inch cubes
½ cup chicken stock
Salt and ground black pepper to taste
1½ tablespoon butter
1½ tablespoon bread crumbs

1. Wash the Brussels sprouts and remove the outer leaves, then cut into halves.
2. In the Instant pot, combine the potatoes, sprouts, stock, salt and pepper. Stir well.
3. Select MANUAL and cook at HIGH pressure for 5 minutes.
4. When the timer goes off, use a Quick Release. Carefully open the lid.
5. Select the SAUTÉ setting; add the butter and bread crumbs to the pot. Mix well and serve.

Colorful Bell Peppery Dish

Prep time: 10 minutes | Cook time: 14 minutes | Serves 4

1 tablespoon extra virgin olive oil
1 red onion, sliced
2 red bell peppers, sliced thinly
2 green bell pepper, sliced thinly
1 yellow bell peppers, sliced thinly
2 tomatoes, chopped
Salt and ground black pepper to taste
2 cloves garlic, chopped
1 bunch parsley, finely chopped

1. Select the SAUTÉ setting on the Instant Pot and heat the oil.
2. Add the onion and sauté for 3 minutes.
3. Add the bell peppers, stir and sauté for another 5 minutes.
4. Add the tomatoes and sprinkle with salt and pepper. Mix well. Close and lock the lid.
5. Press the CANCEL button to reset the cooking program, then press the MANUAL button and set the cooking time for 6 minutes at HIGH pressure.
6. Once pressure cooking is complete, select CANCEL and use a Quick Release. Carefully unlock the lid.
7. Transfer the veggies to a serving bowl and add the garlic and parsley. Stir well. Serve.

Cauliflower Patties with Almond and Cheese

Prep time: 5 minutes | Cook time: 5 minutes | Serves 4

1½ cups water
1 cauliflower head, chopped
1 cup ground almonds
1 cup vegan cheese, shredded
Salt and ground black pepper, to taste
2 tablespoon olive oil

1. Pour the water into the Instant Pot and insert a steamer basket. Put the cauliflower in to the basket.
2. Close and lock the lid. Select MANUAL and cook at HIGH pressure for 5 minutes. Once timer goes off, use a Quick Release. Carefully unlock the lid.
3. Place the cauliflower in a food processor and ground it. Add the almonds and cheese. Season with salt and pepper. Mix well.
4. Shape the mixture into oval patties each ½ inch thick. Carefully pour the water out of the pot and completely dry the pot before replacing it.
5. Select the SAUTÉ setting on the Instant Pot and heat the oil. Add the patties and cook on both sides until golden. You may have to do it in two batches. Serve.

Creamy Artichoke, Zucchini and Garlic

Prep time: 10 minutes | Cook time: 12 minutes | Serves 6 to 8

2 tablespoon olive oil
8 cloves garlic, minced
2 medium zucchinis, sliced thin
1 large artichoke hearts, cleaned and sliced
½ cup whipping cream
½ cup vegetable broth
Salt and ground black pepper, to taste

1. Preheat the Instant Pot by selecting SAUTÉ. Add and heat the oil. Add the garlic and sauté for 2 minutes, until fragrant.
2. Add the zucchinis, artichoke hearts, broth, and cream. Season with salt and pepper. Stir well. Close and lock the lid.
3. Press the CANCEL button to stop the SAUTE function, then select the MANUAL setting and set the cooking time for 10 minutes at high pressure.
4. Once pressure cooking is complete, select CANCEL and use a Quick Release. Carefully unlock the lid. Serve.

Baked Garlicky Asparagus with Parmesan

Prep time: 5 minutes | Cook time: 8 minutes | Serves 2 to 4

1 cup water
1 pound (454 g) asparagus, trimmed
    (1 inch of the bottom)
3 tablespoon butter
2 cloves garlic, chopped
Salt and ground black pepper, to
    taste
3 tablespoon parmesan cheese,
    grated

1. Pour the water into the Instant Pot and set a steam rack in the pot.
2. Place the asparagus on a tin foil, add butter and garlic. Sprinkle with salt and pepper.
3. Fold over the foil and seal the asparagus inside so the foil doesn't come open.
4. Put the asparagus on the rack. Close and lock the lid.
5. Select MANUAL and cook at HIGH pressure for 8 minutes.
6. When the timer beeps, use a Quick Release. Carefully unlock the lid.
7. Unwrap the foil packet and transfer the asparagus to a serving plate. Sprinkle with cheese and serve.

Corn on the Cob

Prep time: 5 minutes | Cook time: 3 minutes | Serves 2 to 4

6 ears corn
1 cup water
6 tablespoon butter
Salt, to taste

1. Shuck the corn husks and rinse off the corn. Cut off the pointy ends. Add the water to the Instant Pot.
2. Arrange the corn vertically, with the larger end in the water. If the ear is too tall break it in half.
3. Close and lock the lid. Select MANUAL and cook at HIGH pressure for 3 minutes.
4. Once timer goes off, use a Quick Release. Carefully unlock the lid. Transfer the corn to a serving bowl. Serve with butter and salt.

Balsamic Sweet Carrot with Potato

Prep time: 10 minutes | Cook time: 12 minutes | Serves 4

1 and ½ pounds (680 g) carrots,
    peeled and sliced
½ teaspoon allspice, ground
½ teaspoon cumin, ground
2 sweet potatoes, cubed
1 tablespoon avocado oil
A pinch of salt and black pepper
1 cup water
1 tablespoon coconut sugar

1. In your instant pot, combine the carrots with the potatoes, allspice, cumin, salt, pepper and the water, put the lid on and cook on High for 12 minutes.
2. Release the pressure fast for 5 minutes, transfer the veggies to a bowl, add the rest of the ingredients, toss, divide between plates and serve as a side dish.

Lime-Orange Brussels Sprouts

Prep time: 10 minutes | Cook time: 8 minutes | Serves 6

1 and ½ pounds (680 g) Brussels
    sprouts, halved
A pinch of salt and black pepper
¼ cup orange juice
1 teaspoon orange zest, grated
1 teaspoon lime zest, grated
1 tablespoon olive oil

1. In your instant pot, combine all the ingredients, toss, put the lid on and cook on High for 8 minutes.
2. Release the pressure naturally for 10 minutes, divide the mix between plates and serve.

Chapter 11 Salads and Wraps

Lime Chicken Salad

Prep time: 15 minutes | Cook time: 5 hours | Serves 4

1 tablespoon minced fresh cilantro
1 teaspoon grated lime zest
¼ cup fresh lime juice
½ teaspoon salt
1 medium onion, cut into wedges
1½ pounds (680 g) bone-in chicken thighs, skin removed
1 tablespoon chili powder
1 teaspoon ground cumin
2 tablespoons extra-virgin olive oil
8 cups torn romaine lettuce
1 medium tomato, chopped
1 avocado, halved, pitted, peeled, and thinly sliced
Chopped fresh cilantro, for serving (optional)

1. In a small bowl, combine the cilantro, lime zest, lime juice, and salt until well blended. Divide the lime juice mixture into two small bowls; set aside.
2. On a 6-quart Instant Pot. Lock the lid in place. Select Manual and cook at high pressure for 15 minutes. Use natural release for 5 minutes, then quick release.
3. Meanwhile, whisk the olive oil into the reserved lime juice mixture until well combined.
4. Layer the lettuce, chicken, onions, tomato, and avocado on serving plates. Drizzle with the dressing and top with cilantro, if desired.

Pork and Lime-Cilantro Salad

Prep time: 20 minutes | Cook time: 5 hours | Serves 4

Pork:
2 teaspoons chili powder
½ teaspoon salt
¼ teaspoon ground cumin
¼ teaspoon black pepper
Dash cayenne pepper
1 Whole30-compliant pork tenderloin (about 1¼ pounds / 567 g), trimmed
½ cup Whole30-compliant chicken broth

Salad:
½ cup Whole30-compliant mayonnaise
½ teaspoon grated lime zest
1 tablespoon fresh lime juice
2 tablespoons chopped fresh cilantro
6 cups chopped butterhead lettuce
1 medium avocado, halved, pitted, peeled, and diced
1 cup grape tomatoes, halved
¼ cup sliced green onions

1. Make the pork: In a small bowl, combine the chili powder, salt, cumin, pepper, and cayenne; sprinkle over the pork. Add the pork to a 6-quart Instant Pot. Pour the broth around the pork.
2. Lock the lid in place. Select Manual and cook at high pressure for 15 minutes. Use natural release for 5 minutes, then quick release. Transfer the pork to a cutting board; cut into ½-inch slices. Discard the cooking liquid.
3. Make the salad: In a small bowl, combine the mayonnaise, lime zest, lime juice, and cilantro. If the dressing is too thick, stir in water, 1 teaspoon at a time, to reach desired consistency. Arrange the lettuce on plates. Top with the pork, avocado, tomatoes, and green onions. Spoon the dressing on top. Season with additional pepper, if desired.

Bacon, Egg, and Veggie Salad with Walnuts

Prep time: 10 minutes | Cook time: 15 minutes | Serves 4

½ cup slivered red onion

⅓ cup cider vinegar

½ teaspoon coarse salt

6 strips Whole30-compliant bacon, chopped

1 to 1¼ pounds (454- to 567-g) sweet potatoes, peeled and cut into 1-inch cubes

8 large eggs

2 teaspoons Whole30-compliant coarse-grain mustard

½ cup avocado oil or walnut oil

6 cups arugula, tough stems trimmed

½ cup chopped walnuts, toasted

1. In a small bowl, toss together the onion, vinegar, and ¼ teaspoon of the salt. Cover and let stand at room temperature while preparing the salad.
2. On a 6-quart Instant Pot, select Sauté and adjust to Normal/Medium. Add the bacon. Cook, stirring occasionally, until the bacon is crisp, about 8 minutes. Press Cancel. Use a slotted spoon to transfer the bacon to paper towels to drain. Crumble the bacon when cool enough to handle.
3. Carefully pour 1 cup water into the bacon grease in the pot. Add the sweet potatoes and place the eggs on the potatoes (the eggs should not touch each other). Lock the lid in place.
4. Select Manual and cook on high pressure for 5 minutes. Use quick release.
5. Meanwhile, combine water and ice in a large bowl to fill halfway. Carefully transfer the eggs to the ice water to cool, about 10 minutes. Use a slotted spoon to transfer the sweet potatoes to another large bowl; set aside. Peel the eggs and thinly slice or cut into halves or quarters.
6. Drain the onion, reserving the vinegar. In a medium bowl, whisk together ¼ cup of the vinegar, the mustard, and remaining ¼ teaspoon salt. Slowly whisk in the oil until the dressing is well combined and thickened. Drizzle the potatoes with about ¼ cup of the dressing. Toss gently to coat.
7. To serve, divide the arugula among four serving plates. Top with the sweet potatoes, eggs, drained onion, and bacon. Drizzle with the remaining dressing. Sprinkle with the walnuts.

Warm Chicken Thighs Romaine Salad

Prep time: 20 minutes | Cook time: 4 hours | Serves 4

4 green onions

2½ pounds (1.1 kg) (1.1 kg) bone-in chicken thighs, skin removed

½ cup Whole30-compliant chicken broth

3 cloves garlic, minced

1 medium red bell pepper, diced

2 stalks celery, thinly sliced

1 tablespoon Whole30-compliant Dijon mustard

2 tablespoons cider vinegar

½ cup Whole30-compliant mayonnaise

1 (16-ounce / 454-g) package hearts of romaine, chopped

1. Thinly slice the green onions; separate the white bottoms from the green tops. In a 6-quart Instant Pot, combine the green onion whites, chicken, broth, and garlic.
2. Lock the lid in place. Select Manual and cook at high pressure for 20 minutes. Use quick release. Add the bell pepper and celery to the pot. Lock the lid in place. Select Manual and cook at high pressure for 3 minutes. Use quick release. Using a slotted spoon, transfer the chicken, pepper, and celery to a large bowl.
3. Let the chicken cool slightly. Remove the chicken from the bones; discard the bones. Use two forks to shred the chicken. Stir the mustard, vinegar, and mayonnaise into the shredded chicken.
4. Arrange the lettuce on four plates; top with the warm chicken salad. Sprinkle with the reserved sliced green onion tops.

Chimichurri Pork Shoulder and Cabbage Salad

Prep time: 30 minutes | Cook time: 9 hours | Serves 6

1 teaspoon salt

1 teaspoon garlic powder

1 teaspoon ground cumin

1 teaspoon black pepper

2½ to 3 pounds (1.1 to 1.4 kg) boneless pork shoulder, trimmed and cut into 3 pieces

1 cup packed fresh cilantro, large stems removed, plus extra for serving

1 cup packed fresh flat-leaf parsley, large stems removed, plus extra for serving

¼ cup chopped shallots

3 cloves garlic, chopped

¼ cup plus 3 tablespoons extra-virgin olive oil

3 tablespoons white wine vinegar

¼ teaspoon red pepper flakes

8 cups coarsely shredded cored savoy or green cabbage

1 cup purchased shredded carrots

½ cup thinly sliced green onion tops

½ cup unsulfured golden raisins

3 tablespoons fresh lemon juice

3 tablespoons extra-virgin olive oil

½ cup chopped walnuts or pecans, toasted

1. In a small bowl, combine ½ teaspoon of the salt, the garlic powder, cumin, and pepper. Sprinkle all over the pork pieces; rub in with your fingers. Place the pork in a 6-quart Instant Pot. Lock the lid in place. Select Manual and cook at high pressure for 30 minutes. Use natural release for 10 minutes, then quick release.
2. Transfer the pork to a cutting board; cool for about 10 minutes. Using two forks, coarsely shred the pork; transfer to a large bowl.
3. Meanwhile, in a blender or food processor, combine the cilantro, parsley, shallots, garlic, ¼ cup of the olive oil, the vinegar, and red pepper flakes. Cover and blend or process until almost smooth. Pour over the shredded pork and stir to combine. Set aside.
4. In a large bowl, toss together the cabbage, carrots, green onion tops, and raisins. In a small bowl, whisk together the remaining 3 tablespoons olive oil, remaining ½ teaspoon salt, and the lemon juice. Pour over the cabbage salad and toss to coat. Stir in the pork. Sprinkle with the walnuts and additional cilantro and/or parsley.

Chicken Breast and Cucumber Salad

Prep time: 10 minutes | Cook time: 20 minutes | Serves 4

2 chicken breasts, skinless, boneless and halved
1 tablespoon sweet paprika
1 cup chicken stock
1 tablespoon olive oil
1 yellow onion, chopped
½ teaspoon cinnamon powder
2 cucumbers, sliced
1 avocado, peeled, pitted and cubed
1 tomato, cubed
1 tablespoon cilantro, chopped

1. Set instant pot on Sauté mode, add the oil, heat it up, add the onion and the meat and brown for 5 minutes.
2. Add the paprika, stock and the cinnamon, put the lid on and cook on High for 15 minutes.
3. Release the pressure naturally for 10 minutes, and divide the chicken between plates.
4. In a bowl, mix the cucumbers with the avocado, tomato and cilantro, toss, divide the mix next to the chicken and serve.

Dill Egg and Potato Salad

Prep time: 10 minutes | Cook time: 5 minutes | Serves 2 to 4

1½ cups water
6 russet potatoes, peeled and diced
4 large eggs
1 cup mayonnaise
2 tablespoons fresh parsley, chopped
¼ cup onion, chopped
1 tablespoon dill pickle juice
1 tablespoon mustard
Pinch of salt
Pinch of ground black pepper

1. Pour the water into the Instant Pot and insert a steamer basket.
2. Place the potatoes and eggs in the basket.
3. Close and lock the lid. Select the MANUAL setting and set the cooking time for 5 minutes at HIGH pressure.
4. Once pressure cooking is complete, use a Quick Release. Carefully unlock the lid.
5. Transfer the eggs to the bowl of cold water and cool for 2 to 3 minutes.
6. In a medium bowl, combine the mayonnaise, parsley, onion, dill pickle juice, and mustard. Mix well. Add salt and pepper.
7. Peel and slice the eggs. Toss the potatoes and eggs in the bowl. Stir and serve.

Tropically Chicken and Pineapple Salad

Prep time: 10 minutes | Cook time: 2 hours | Serves 4

1½ pounds (680 g) boneless, skinless chicken breasts
1 (20-ounce / 567-g) can crushed pineapple in 100% pineapple juice, drained
1 green bell pepper, diced
1 red onion, finely chopped
1 clove garlic, minced
2 tablespoons coconut aminos
½ teaspoon salt
¼ teaspoon black pepper
8 chard leaves, stems removed and leaves sliced into ribbons
1 avocado, halved, pitted, peeled, and sliced
1 jalapeño, seeded, if desired, and sliced
Lime wedges

1. Cut the chicken crosswise into 1-inch-wide strips. In a a 6-quart Instant Pot, combine the chicken, pineapple, bell pepper, onion, garlic, coconut aminos, salt, and pepper. Turn the chicken to coat. Lock the lid in place. Select Manual and cook at high pressure for 8 minutes. Use natural release for 3 minutes, then quick release.
2. Transfer the chicken to a cutting board. Use two forks to shred the chicken, then return to the slow cooker and stir.
3. Divide the chard among four bowls; top with the chicken mixture, avocado, and jalapeño. Serve with lime wedges.

Oregano Chicken Breast and Kale Salad

Prep time: 20 minutes | Cook time: 6 hours | Serves 6

Chicken:

3 bone-in, skin-on chicken breast halves
3 sprigs fresh oregano
2 teaspoons grated orange zest
2 cloves garlic, minced
1½ teaspoons dried oregano
½ teaspoon salt
½ teaspoon black pepper
¼ cup fresh orange juice
2 tablespoons extra-virgin olive oil

Dressing:

2 tablespoons red wine vinegar
1 tablespoon fresh orange juice
½ teaspoon salt
½ teaspoon black pepper
3 tablespoons extra-virgin olive oil
½ cup thinly sliced red onion
1 bunch kale, stems removed and torn into bite-size pieces

1. Make the chicken: Use your fingers to loosen the skin from the meat of the chicken but do not remove the skin. Place an oregano sprig underneath the skin of each breast half. In a small bowl, combine the orange zest, minced garlic, oregano, salt, and pepper; rub over the chicken. Place the chicken in a 6-quart Instant Pot. Drizzle with the orange juice, then the olive oil.
2. Lock the lid in place. Select Manual and cook at high pressure for 30 minutes. Use natural release for 10 minutes, then quick release. Remove the chicken; let cool until easy to handle. Remove the chicken from the bones; discard the skin, bones, and herb sprigs. Use two forks to shred the chicken. Moisten the chicken with the cooking liquid.
3. Make the dressing: Meanwhile, in a small bowl, combine the vinegar, orange juice, salt, and pepper. Whisk in the olive oil. Add the onion; cover and let stand for at least 1 hour.
4. Place the kale in a large bowl. Drizzle with the dressing and toss to coat. Add the chicken and toss to combine (the kale will wilt slightly).

Green Beans and Potato Salad

Prep time: 10 minutes | Cook time: 6 minutes | Serves 4 to 6

1 ounce (28 g) dried porcini mushrooms, soaked
  overnight and rinsed
2 pounds (907 g) potatoes, sliced to 1 inch thick
2 pounds (907 g) green beans, trimmed and cleaned
Boiling water as needed
Salt and ground black pepper, to taste
1 tablespoon olive oil
1 tablespoon balsamic vinegar

1. Add the mushrooms, potatoes, and beans to the Instant Pot.
2. Add water to cover the vegetables.
3. Close and secure the lid. Select the MANUAL setting and set the cooking time for 6 minutes at HIGH pressure.
4. Once pressure cooking is complete, use a Quick Release.
5. Transfer the vegetables into a salad bowl and drain the water.
6. Add the salt, pepper, olive oil and balsamic vinegar. Stir well until fully coated. Serve.

Salmon and Greens

Salad

Prep time: 15 minutes | Cook time: 3 minutes | Serves 4

1 cup cider vinegar
½ cup thinly sliced radishes
½ cup matchstick carrots
½ cup thinly sliced cucumber
½ teaspoon salt
4 (4-ounce / 113-g) skinless salmon fillets
Cracked black pepper, to taste
2 tablespoons avocado oil
2 tablespoons fresh lemon juice
3 tablespoons Whole30-compliant hot sauce
1 (5-ounce / 142-g) package mixed salad greens
2 tablespoons chopped fresh chives

1. In a small bowl, combine the vinegar, radishes, carrots, cucumber, and ¼ teaspoon of the salt. Let sit while preparing the salmon.
2. Add the rack and 1 cup water to a 6-quart Instant Pot. Season the salmon with remaining ¼ teaspoon salt and the pepper. Place the salmon on the rack. Lock the lid in place.
3. Select Manual and cook on high pressure for 3 minutes. Use quick release. Remove the salmon.
4. For the dressing, whisk together the oil, lemon juice, and hot sauce in another small bowl. Drain the vegetables; discard the vinegar. Arrange the greens on serving plates and top with the vegetables. Use a fork to break the salmon into chunks. Add the salmon to the salads. Drizzle with the dressing and sprinkle with the chives.

Mediterranean-Style Chicken Salad

Prep time: 15 minutes | Cook time: 5 hours | Serves 4

Dressing:

½ cup extra-virgin olive oil

¼ cup fresh lemon juice

2 cloves garlic, minced

2 teaspoons Whole30-compliant Italian seasoning

¼ teaspoon salt

Chicken and Salad:

1 pound (454 g) bone-in, skinless chicken thighs

1 medium red onion, cut into wedges

8 cups torn romaine lettuce

1 red bell pepper, chopped

1 medium cucumber, chopped

¼ cup sliced pitted Whole30-compliant Kalamata olives

1. Make the dressing: In a small bowl, combine the olive oil, lemon juice, garlic, Italian seasoning, and salt until well blended; set aside.
2. Make the chicken: In a 6-quart Instant Pot, layer the chicken and onion. Pour half the dressing over the chicken and onions. Cover and refrigerate the remaining dressing.
3. Lock the lid in place. Select Manual and cook at high pressure for 15 minutes. Use natural release for 5 minutes, then quick release. Transfer the chicken and onions to a cutting board. Using two forks, pull the chicken apart into large shreds.
4. Arrange the lettuce, chicken and onion, bell pepper, cucumber, and olives on serving plates. Drizzle with the reserved dressing.

Asian Sirloin Steak Lettuce Wraps

Prep time: 15 minutes | Cook time: 15 minutes | Serves 4

2 tablespoons olive or avocado oil

2 pounds (907 g) top sirloin steak or stew meat

½ cup coconut aminos

¼ cup beef stock

2 tablespoons rice vinegar

3 tablespoons coconut sugar

2 tablespoons sriracha or chili garlic sauce

2 teaspoons sesame oil

1 teaspoon ground ginger

2 tablespoons arrowroot powder

2 tablespoons water

1 head romaine lettuce

1 cup matchstick-sliced carrot

⅓ cup diced green onion

¼ cup chopped fresh cilantro (optional)

1. Select sauté on the Instant Pot. Once hot, coat the bottom of the Instant Pot with the olive oil. Place the meat in the pot and brown on all sides. This should take 3 to 4 minutes. Select cancel.
2. In a medium bowl, whisk together the soy sauce, beef stock, vinegar, coconut sugar, sriracha, sesame oil and ginger. Pour the soy sauce mixture over the beef.
3. Secure the lid with the steam vent in the sealed position. Select manual or pressure, and cook on high pressure for 10 minutes.
4. Use a natural release for 15 minutes, then release any remaining steam.
5. After removing the lid, in a small bowl, stir together the arrowroot starch and water and pour into the pot. Select the sauté function and let the liquid come to a quick boil, then select cancel and let the sauce thicken.
6. Assemble the lettuce wraps by adding the beef, carrot, green onion and cilantro (if using).

Beet and Grapefruit Salad

Prep time: 10 minutes | Cook time: 20 minutes | Serves 8

6 medium fresh beets (about 2-pound / 907-g)

1½ cups water

¼ cup extra virgin olive oil

3 tablespoons lemon juice

2 tablespoons cider vinegar

¼ teaspoon salt

¼ teaspoon pepper

2 large ruby red grapefruit, peeled and sectioned

2 small red onions, halved and thinly sliced

1. Scrub beets, trimming tops to 1 in. Place beets on trivet of a 6-qt. electric pressure cooker. Add 1½ cups water. Lock lid; make sure vent is closed. Select manual setting; adjust pressure to high and set time to 20 minutes.
2. When finished cooking, let pressure release naturally before opening; remove beets and cool completely before peeling, halving and thinly slicing them. Place in a serving bowl. Whisk together next six ingredients. Pour over beets; add grapefruit and onion. Toss gently to coat.

Peppers and Egg Salad Wraps

Prep time: 15 minutes | Cook time: 5 minutes | Serves 4

1 cup water
8 large eggs
½ cup mayonnaise
1 chipotle pepper (from a can of chipotle peppers in adobo)
½ red bell pepper, seeded and diced
½ poblano pepper, diced
1 jalapeño pepper, minced
¼ cup chopped fresh cilantro
¼ cup chopped green onion
Salt and freshly ground black pepper, to taste
4 large lettuce leaves
4 slices tomato, halved

1. Pour the water into the Instant Pot and insert the steam trivet. Carefully place the eggs on the trivet.
2. Secure the lid with the steam vent in the sealed position. Press manual and immediately adjust the timer to 5 minutes. Check that the display light is beneath high pressure.
3. Once the timer sounds, allow the pressure to release naturally for 10 minutes, then quick release the pressure and carefully remove the lid. Run the eggs under cold water until cool, then peel.
4. In a medium bowl, mix together the mayonnaise and chipotle pepper. Stir in the bell, poblano and jalapeño peppers, cilantro and green onion.
5. Chop the eggs and gently fold them into the mayonnaise mixture. Season with salt and pepper.
6. Divide the egg salad among the lettuce leaves, then top with the tomato slices.

Blt Chicken Breast Salad

Prep time: 10 minutes | Cook time: 6 minutes | Serves 4

½ pound (227 g) bacon
1 cup water or chicken stock
1½ pounds (680 g) boneless, skinless chicken breast, cut into bite-size pieces
1 cup cherry tomatoes, halved
½ cup mayonnaise
Coarse salt, to taste
Freshly ground pepper, to taste
4 cups spring mix lettuce

1. Press sauté to preheat the Instant Pot. When the word "hot" appears on the display, add the bacon. Cook until the bacon is browned and crispy, then remove it with a slotted spoon and place on paper towels to drain any excess fat. Discard the drippings but do not wipe clean.
2. Add the water or chicken stock to the pot, taking care to scrape up any browned bits from the bottom of the pot. Add the chicken.
3. Secure the lid with the steam vent in the sealed position. Press manual and immediately adjust the timer to 6 minutes. Check that the display light is beneath high pressure.
4. When the timer sounds, quick release the pressure and carefully remove the lid. Remove the chicken and allow to cool completely.
5. In a large bowl, mix together the chicken, tomatoes and mayonnaise. Crumble the bacon and gently fold into the chicken mixture. Season with salt and pepper.
6. Place 1 cup (55 g) of lettuce on each of the four plates. Evenly divide the chicken salad and place on top of the lettuce.

Chicken Breast and Lime-Cilantro Salad

Prep time: 10 minutes | Cook time: 6 minutes | Serves 4

½ cup chicken stock
2 pounds (907 g) boneless, skinless chicken breast
½ cup chopped red onion
2 cloves garlic, minced
1 cup mayonnaise
1 poblano pepper, chopped
1 red bell pepper, seeded and chopped
Juice of 1 lime
½ cup chopped fresh cilantro

1. Pour the chicken stock into the Instant Pot, then add the chicken breast.
2. Secure the lid with the steam vent in the sealed position. Press manual and immediately adjust the timer to 6 minutes. Check that the display light is beneath high pressure.
3. When the timer sounds, quick release the pressure and carefully remove the lid.
4. In a medium bowl, mix together the red onion, garlic, mayonnaise, poblano and bell peppers, lime juice and cilantro. Remove the chicken from the pot, chop the chicken and mix it with the sauce.
5. Refrigerate for at least 1 hour before serving.

Prosciutto Wrapped Asparagus

Prep time: 5 minutes | Cook time: 3 minutes | Serves 2 to 4

1½ cups water
1 pound (454 g) asparagus
10 ounces (283 g) prosciutto, sliced

1. Wash asparagus and trim off bottom of stems by about 1 inch.
2. Prepare the Instant Pot by adding the water to the pot and placing the steam rack in it.
3. Wrap the prosciutto slices around the asparagus spears.
4. Place the un-wrapped asparagus on the rack, and then place the prosciutto-wrapped spears on top.
5. Close and lock the lid. Select MANUAL and cook at HIGH pressure for 3 minutes.
6. When the timer goes off, let the pressure Release Naturally for 5 minutes, then release any remaining steam manually. Open the lid.
7. Serve.

Per Serving
calories: | fat: g | protein: g | carbs: g | fiber: g | sodium: g

Simple Broccoli Salad

Prep time: 5 minutes | Cook time: 15 minutes | Serves 4

1 pound (454 g) broccoli florets
Salt and black pepper to the taste
2 tablespoons olive oil
½ cup chicken stock
1 teaspoon thyme, dried
1 teaspoon sweet paprika

1. In your instant pot, combine all the ingredients, put the lid on and cook on High for 15 minutes.
2. Release the pressure naturally for 10 minutes, divide the mix between plates and serve as a side dish.

Per Serving
calories: 187 | fat: 7g | protein: 5g | carbs: 5g | fiber: 3g | sodium: g

Broccoli and Orange Salad

Prep time: 10 minutes | Cook time: 7 minutes | Serves 4

1 pound (454 g) broccoli, florets separated
2 oranges, peeled and cut into segments
Zest of 1 orange, grated
Juice of 1 orange
1 cup water
1 red chili pepper, chopped
A pinch of salt and black pepper
3 tablespoons avocado oil

1. Put the water in your instant pot, add steamer basket, add the broccoli inside, put the lid on and cook on High for 7 minutes.
2. Release the pressure naturally for 10 minutes, drain the broccoli, transfer it to a bowl, add the rest of the ingredients, toss and serve as a side salad.

Per Serving
calories: 142 | fat: 4g | protein: 5g | carbs: 4g | fiber: 2g | sodium: g

Chapter 12 Soups, Stews, and Noodle Bowls

Polish Kielbasa and Cabbage Soup

Prep time: 15 minutes | Cook time: 32 minutes | Serves 6

4 slices Whole30-compliant bacon, chopped
1 medium yellow onion, chopped
½ cup chopped celery
6 cups Whole30-compliant chicken
1 (10-ounce / 283-g) package shredded cabbage
3 medium carrots, peeled and chopped
1 large russet potato, peeled and cubed
½ teaspoon dried thyme
¼ teaspoon salt
¼ teaspoon white pepper
1 bay leaf
2 tablespoons cider vinegar
1 (12- to 14-ounce / 340- to 397-g) package Whole30-compliant
    kielbasa, sliced
Fresh dill, for serving

1. On a 6-quart Instant Pot, select Sauté and adjust to Normal/ Medium. Add the bacon and cook until crisp, about 5 minutes. Use a slotted spoon to transfer the bacon to paper towels. Add the onion and celery to the bacon drippings in the pot. Cook, stirring occasionally, until softened, 2 to 3 minutes. Add the broth, cabbage, carrots, potato, thyme, salt, pepper, bay leaf, and vinegar. Lock the lid in place.
2. Select Manual and cook on high pressure for 20 minutes. Use natural release.
3. Remove and discard the bay leaf. Add the kielbasa. Cover and let stand until heated through, about 5 minutes. Sprinkle servings with the crumbled bacon and fresh dill.

Pork Shoulder and Carrot Noodle Bowls

Prep time: 15 minutes | Cook time: 15 minutes | Serves 4

2½ pounds (1.1 kg) (1.1 kg) Whole30-compliant boneless pork
    shoulder, trimmed and cut into 1-inch pieces
¾ teaspoon salt
½ teaspoon black pepper
2 tablespoons coconut oil
1 (13½-ounce / 383-g) can Whole30-compliant coconut milk
¼ cup Whole30-compliant green curry paste
1 small onion, chopped
2 medium red, yellow, or green bell peppers, chopped
1 piece (1 inch) fresh ginger, peeled and grated
3 cloves garlic, minced
1 (12-ounce / 340-g) package frozen carrot spirals or 4 large carrots,
    spiralized, long noodles snipped
¼ cup unsweetened shredded coconut, lightly toasted
¼ cup chopped fresh cilantro or basil
1 lime, cut into wedges

1. Sprinkle the pork with the salt and pepper. In a 6-quart Instant Pot, use the Sauté setting and heat 1 tablespoon of the coconut oil. Add half the pork and cook until browned, about 5 minutes. Transfer the pork to a plate. Repeat with the remaining 1 tablespoon oil and pork. Return all the pork to the pot. Add the coconut milk, curry paste, onion, bell pepper, ginger, and garlic.
2. Lock the lid in place. Select Manual and cook for 10 minutes on high pressure. Use natural release. Stir in the carrot noodles. Cover and let sit for 5 minutes to soften the noodles.
3. Spoon the curry into bowls, top with lightly toasted coconut and cilantro or basil, and serve with lime wedges.

Hearty Chicken and Carrot Stew

Prep time: 30 minutes | Cook time: 6 hours | Serves 4

1 medium onion, cut into wedges
2 cloves garlic, minced
4 slices Whole30-compliant bacon, chopped
4 medium carrots, peeled and cut into 1-inch pieces
1 large leek, white part only, sliced
12 small red potatoes (about 12 ounces / 340 g)
Grated zest and juice of 1 lemon
½ cup Whole30-compliant chicken broth
1 tablespoon tapioca flour
1 teaspoon salt
½ teaspoon coarsely ground black pepper
8 meaty bone-in chicken pieces (breast halves, thighs, and drumsticks), skin removed
2 tablespoons extra-virgin olive oil
2 teaspoons herbes de Provence
2 tablespoons Whole30-compliant Dijon mustard
1 cup Whole30-compliant Kalamata olives or other black olives
Fresh tarragon leaves, for serving

1. In a a 6-quart Instant Pot, combine the onion, garlic, bacon, and leek. In a small bowl, stir together the lemon juice, broth, and tapioca flour; stir into the slow cooker. In another small bowl, combine the lemon zest, salt, and pepper. Coat the chicken with the olive oil and rub with the salt mixture. Add to the Instant Pot. Sprinkle the herbes de Provence over the chicken.
2. Lock the lid in place. Select Manual and cook at high pressure for 45 minutes. Use natural release for 10 minutes, then quick release.
3. Remove the chicken. Stir in the carrots and potatoes. Lock the lid in place. Select Manual and cook at high pressure for 5 minutes. Use quick release. Return the chicken to the pot and stir the mustard and olives into the cooking liquid. Ladle some of the cooking liquid over the chicken. Sprinkle with fresh tarragon leaves and serve

Moringa Chicken Breast Soup

Prep time: 10 minutes | Cook time: 18 minutes | Serves 8

1½ pounds (680 g) chicken breasts
Salt and pepper, to taste
2 cloves of garlic, minced
1 onion, chopped
5 cups water
1 thumb-size ginger
1 cup tomatoes, chopped
2 cups moringa leaves or kale leaves

1. Place all ingredients in the Instant Pot except for the moringa leaves.
2. Close the lid and press the Poultry button.
3. Adjust the cooking time to 15 minutes.
4. Do natural pressure release.
5. Once the lid is open, press the Sauté button.
6. Stir in the moringa leaves and simmer for 3 minutes.

Brazilian Fish and Shrimp Stew

Prep time: 20 minutes | Cook time: 25 minutes | Serves 4

For the Seasoning and Seafood:
1 teaspoon smoked paprika
½ teaspoon salt
½ teaspoon garlic powder
½ teaspoon ground cumin
¼ teaspoon ground coriander
1 pound (454 g) red snapper, halibut, or cod fillets, cut into 1-inch pieces
1 pound (454 g) peeled and deveined medium shrimp

For the Stew:
2 tablespoons extra-virgin olive oil
1 medium yellow onion, chopped
2 cloves garlic, minced
1 red bell pepper, sliced into matchsticks
1 (10-ounce / 283-g) package frozen sweet potatoes
1 (14-ounce / 397-g) can Whole30-compliant fire-roasted diced tomatoes, undrained
1 (13½-ounce / 383-g) can Whole30-compliant coconut milk
½ teaspoon red pepper flakes
2 teaspoons sweet paprika
1 lime, cut into wedges

1. Season the seafood: In a small bowl, combine the smoked paprika, salt, garlic powder, cumin, and coriander. Place the cod and shrimp in a large bowl and sprinkle with the seasoning. Set aside.
2. Make the stew: On a 6-quart Instant Pot, select Sauté and adjust to Normal/Medium. Add the olive oil to the pot. When it's hot, add the onion and garlic and cook, stirring occasionally, until the onion is softened, about 2 minutes. Press Cancel.
3. Add the bell pepper, sweet potatoes, tomatoes, coconut milk, red pepper flakes, and sweet paprika; stir. Add the fish and shrimp to the pot. Stir gently. Lock the lid in place.
4. Select Manual and cook on high pressure for 2 minutes. Use quick release.
5. Serve the stew with lime wedges.

Instant Pot Chicken Soup

Prep time: 10 minutes | Cook time: 30 minutes | Serves 12

1 large onion diced
2 large carrots or 3 small, chopped
1½ cup green beans chopped into 1 inch pieces
4 garlic cloves minced
1 inch ginger minced
4 pounds (1.8 kg) whole chicken preferably pasture raised
2 teaspoon sea salt plus more to taste
Cracked black pepper to taste
5 cups water
Chopped green onions, for garnish

1. Place onion, carrots, green beans, garlic, and ginger in the instant pot.
2. Lay the chicken over the vegetables.
3. Sprinkle with salt and pepper.
4. Pour water over everything.
5. Close the lid of the Instant Pot, then set it to "Soup" on high pressure of 30 minutes.
6. Once the soup is finished, the Instant Pot will beep a few times. Wait about 30 minutes for the pressure to go down naturally until you can open the lid.
7. Take out the chicken and debone. You can save the bones to make bone broth.
8. Shred the meat and place back in the instant pot. Stir.
9. Taste and add more salt and pepper, if needed.
10. Serve with chopped green onions sprinkled on top.

Chicken and Sweet Potatoes Stew with Almond

Prep time: 30 minutes | Cook time: 6 hours | Serves 6

1½ pounds (680 g) boneless, skinless chicken thighs, cut into 1½-inch pieces
2 medium sweet potatoes (about 1¼ pounds / 567 g total), peeled and cut into 1½-inch pieces
1 (14½-ounce / 411-g) can Whole30-compliant stewed tomatoes, undrained
1 medium yellow onion, chopped
3 cloves garlic, minced
1 piece (1 inch) fresh ginger, peeled and finely chopped
¼ teaspoon cayenne pepper
2½ cups Whole30-compliant chicken broth
1 bunch collard greens, trimmed and coarsely chopped
¼ cup Whole30-compliant sunflower seed butter
½ cup chopped almonds, toasted
½ cup chopped fresh cilantro or flat-leaf parsley

1. In a 6-quart Instant Pot, combine the chicken, sweet potatoes, tomatoes, onion, garlic, ginger, and cayenne. Add the broth. Lock the lid in place. Select Manual and cook at high pressure for 10 minutes. Use quick release.
2. Remove ½ cup of the cooking liquid and set aside. Add the collard greens, select Sauté and adjust to Less/Low. Simmer, uncovered, for 15 minutes. Whisk the sunflower butter into the reserved cooking liquid until smooth. Stir into the stew.
3. Serve, sprinkled with almonds and cilantro.

Salmon Fillet and Zucchini Stew

Prep time: 10 minutes | Cook time: 6 hours | Serves 3

½ pound (227 g) salmon fillet, cubed
½ tablespoon coconut oil
½ medium onion, chopped
½ garlic clove, minced
½ zucchini, sliced
½ green bell pepper, seeded and cubed
¼ cup tomatoes, chopped
½ cup fish broth
1/8 teaspoon dried oregano, crushed
1/8 teaspoon dried basil, crushed
Salt and ground black pepper, to taste

1. Add all the ingredients to the Instant pot and mix well.
2. Secure the lid and select "Slow Cook" for 6 hours.
3. Keep the pressure release handle to the "venting" position.
4. After complete cooking, stir the stew well.
5. Serve immediately.

Root Vegetable and Beef Stew

Prep time: 25 minutes | Cook time: 6 hours | Serves 4

2 tablespoons extra-virgin olive oil

1½ pounds (680 g) beef stew meat, cut into ¾-inch pieces

4 medium carrots, peeled and diagonally sliced 1 inch thick

8 baby red potatoes, quartered

1 medium yellow onion, cut into thin wedges

2 cloves garlic, minced

½ teaspoon salt

½ teaspoon black pepper

1 bay leaf

2 cups Whole30-compliant beef broth

2 cups Whole30-compliant vegetable juice

2 tablespoons coconut aminos

1. In a 6-quart Instant Pot, selecting Sauté and adjusting to High. Add the beef and cook in batches if necessary, stirring occasionally, until browned on all sides.
2. Add the carrots, potatoes, onion, garlic, salt, pepper, bay leaf, broth, vegetable juice, and coconut aminos; stir to combine. Lock the lid in place. Select Manual and cook at high pressure for 25 minutes. Use natural release for 10 minutes, then quick release.
3. If using the tapioca flour, select Sauté and adjusting to High on the Instant Pot. Remove and discard the bay leaf before serving.

Pulled Pork with Broccoli-Cauliflower Rice

Prep time: 15 minutes | Cook time: 1¼ hours | Serves 6

For the Pork:

2 tablespoons Whole30-compliant za'atar seasoning

1 (3- to 4-pound / 1.4- to 1.8-kg) pork shoulder, trimmed

1 tablespoon extra-virgin olive oil

1 medium yellow onion, chopped

1 serrano chile pepper, seeded and finely chopped

4 Roma (plum) tomatoes, cored and chopped

For the Spiced Broccoli-Cauliflower Rice:

2 (10-ounce / 283-g) packages frozen riced cauliflower and broccoli

1 tablespoon clarified butter or ghee

½ teaspoon ground turmeric

½ teaspoon ground coriander

½ teaspoon ground cumin

¼ teaspoon salt

¼ teaspoon black pepper

Make the Pork
1. Rub the za'atar on all sides of the pork. On a 6-quart Instant Pot, select Sauté and adjust to Normal/Medium. Add the olive oil. When it's hot, add the roast and cook until browned on all sides, about 10 minutes. Remove the roast from the pot. Add the onion and serrano pepper and cook just until softened, about 2 minutes. Add the tomatoes and cook just until softened, about 3 minutes. Return the roast to the pot. Spoon some of the tomato mixture over the roast. Lock the lid in place.
2. Select Manual and cook on high pressure for 60 minutes. Use natural release.

Make the Broccoli-Cauliflower Rice
3. Prepare the riced broccoli and cauliflower according to the package directions. Stir in the butter, turmeric, coriander, and cumin. Sprinkle with the salt and pepper.
4. Remove the pork from the pot. Discard any fat and place the pork in a large bowl. Strain the cooking liquid through a fine-mesh sieve; add the solids to the pork and discard the cooking liquid. Use two forks to shred the pork.
5. Serve the shredded pork over the broccoli-cauliflower rice.

Split Pea Soup with Ham Bone

Prep time: 10 minutes | Cook time: 25 minutes | Serves 4 to 6

2 teaspoons olive oil

1 medium onion, chopped

2 celery ribs, chopped

3 carrots, chopped

6 cups chicken stock

1 Whole30 compliant ham bone

1 pound (454 g) dried split peas

1 bay leaf

Coarse salt, to taste

Freshly ground black pepper, to taste

1. Press sauté to preheat the Instant Pot. When the word "hot" appears on the display, add the olive oil, then the onion, celery and carrots. Cook, stirring occasionally, until the onion is soft, about 5 minutes. Press cancel to turn off the Instant Pot.
2. Add the chicken stock, taking care to scrape up any browned bits from the bottom of the pot. Add the ham bone, split peas and bay leaf.
3. Secure the lid with the steam vent in the sealed position. Press soup and immediately adjust the timer to 20 minutes. Check that the display light is beneath high pressure.
4. Once the timer sounds, allow the pressure to release naturally for 10 minutes, then quick release the pressure and carefully remove the lid. Remove the ham bone, and any meat that fell from the ham bone, from the pot. Remove and discard the bay leaf. Using an immersion blender, puree the soup until smooth. Remove the meat from the ham bone and add it and any other meat that was removed back to the pot. Season well with salt and pepper, then serve.

Sweet Potatoes and Pork Stew

Prep time: 30 minutes | Cook time: 6 hours | Serves 6

2 pounds (907 g) lean ground pork
1 quart Whole30-compliant vegetable broth
3 medium sweet potatoes, peeled and cut into 1-inch pieces
1 Braeburn apple, cored and cut into 1-inch pieces
2 jalapeños, seeded and diced
1 large shallot, minced
1 tablespoon fresh thyme, plus extra for serving
2 teaspoons ground ginger
½ teaspoon salt
½ teaspoon white pepper
Paprika, for serving

1. In a 6-quart Instant Pot, select Sauté and adjust to Normal/Medium to cook the pork until no longer pink, about 10 minutes. Add the broth, sweet potatoes, apple, jalapeños, shallot, thyme, ginger, salt, and white pepper. Lock the lid in place. Select Manual and cook at low pressure for 10 minutes. Use natural release for 5 minutes, then quick release.
2. Use a potato masher or fork to gently mash the sweet potatoes to thicken the stew.
3. Serve, sprinkled with paprika and fresh thyme.

Pork Loin and Veggie Stew

Prep time: 25 minutes | Cook time: 6 hours | Serves 6

1½ pounds (680 g) Whole30-compliant boneless pork loin, cut into 1-inch pieces
½ small butternut squash, peeled and cut into 1-inch pieces (about 2 cups)
3 medium carrots, peeled and cut into ½-inch pieces
2 medium parsnips, peeled and cut into ½-inch pieces
1 medium yellow onion, chopped
2 teaspoons fresh thyme
½ teaspoon salt
½ teaspoon black pepper
4 cups Whole30-compliant chicken broth
Chopped fresh parsley, for serving

1. In a 6-quart Instant Pot, combine the pork, squash, carrots, parsnips, onion, thyme, salt, pepper, and broth. Lock the lid in place. Select Manual and cook at high pressure for 4 minutes. Use natural release for 5 minutes, then quick release.
2. Serve, topped with parsley.

Chicken Breast and Vegetable Soup

Prep time: 10 minutes | Cook time: 9 minutes | Serves 4

2 tablespoons clarified butter or ghee
1½ pounds (680 g) boneless, skinless chicken breasts, cut into 1-inch pieces
1 large yellow onion, chopped
1 teaspoon salt
¼ teaspoon red pepper flakes
4 cups Whole30-compliant chicken broth
1 (14½-ounce / 411.1-g) can Whole30-compliant diced tomatoes, undrained
1 medium zucchini, halved lengthwise and sliced ½ inch thick
2 cloves garlic, minced
1½ teaspoons Whole30-compliant Italian seasoning
2 tablespoons chopped fresh basil

1. On a 6-quart Instant Pot, select Sauté and adjust to Normal/Medium. Add the butter, chicken, onion, salt, and red pepper flakes. Cook, stirring occasionally, until the chicken is opaque, 4 to 5 minutes. Select Cancel. Stir in the broth, tomatoes, zucchini, garlic, and Italian seasoning. Lock the lid in place.
2. Select Manual and cook on high pressure for 5 minutes. Use quick release.
3. Serve the soup topped with the basil.

Pork and Carrot-Noodles Bowls

Prep time: 10 minutes | Cook time: 2¼ hours | Serves 4

½ cup apple cider
½ cup coconut aminos
¼ teaspoon red pepper flakes
1½ pounds (680 g) Whole30-compliant pork tenderloin, trimmed
2 teaspoons Whole30-compliant five-spice powder
½ teaspoon salt
2 tablespoons clarified butter or ghee
1 (12-ounce / 340-g) package frozen carrot noodles or 4 large carrots, peeled and spiralized
2 tablespoons sliced green onion
2 tablespoons chopped fresh cilantro
1 tablespoon sesame seeds, toasted

1. In a 4-quart slow cooker, stir together the apple cider, coconut aminos, and red pepper flakes. Sprinkle the pork with the five-spice powder and salt. Add the pork to slow cooker and turn to coat.
2. Cover and cook on low for 4½ to 5 hours or on high for 2¼ to 2½ hours. Transfer the pork to a cutting board and cut into bite-size strips. Strain the cooking liquid.
3. In a large skillet, heat the butter over medium heat. Add the carrot noodles and cook, stirring occasionally, until tender, 5 to 10 minutes.
4. Serve the pork on the carrot noodles and drizzle with some of the strained cooking liquid. Top with the green onion, cilantro, and sesame seeds. If desired serve with additional coconut aminos.

Beef Chuck Roast and Beet Borscht

Prep time: 10 minutes | Cook time: 20 minutes | Serves 4

1 large bunch red beets with greens
1¼ pounds (567 g) beef chuck roast, trimmed and cut into ½-inch chunks
1 tablespoon extra-virgin olive oil
Salt and freshly ground black pepper, to taste
2½ cups beef broth
1 yellow onion, chopped
1 teaspoon caraway seeds
1 teaspoon dried dill
1 tablespoon balsamic or red wine vinegar
Optional garnish

1. Wash the beets and the greens well. Peel the beets and cut them into ½-inch pieces; set aside. Finely chop the stems and greens (keep them separate) until you have 1 cup of each; set aside.
2. Toss half the beef with the oil and season generously with salt and pepper. Select SAUTÉ and adjust to MORE/HIGH heat. When the pot is hot, add the seasoned beef and cook, stirring occasionally, until well browned, 4 minutes. Press CANCEL.
3. Add the remaining (unbrowned) beef, the broth, beets, beet stems, onions, caraway, and dill to the pot. (You'll add the beet greens at the end of cooking.) Lock on the lid, select the PRESSURE COOK function, and adjust to HIGH pressure for 15 minutes. Make sure the steam valve is in the "Sealing" position. (Or you can SLOW COOK it—see instructions below.)
4. When the cooking time is up, let the pressure release naturally for 10 minutes and then carefully release the remaining pressure. Add the vinegar and beet greens to the pot. Select SAUTÉ and adjust to MORE/HIGH heat. Cook until the soup is simmering and the greens are tender, 1 minute. Press CANCEL. Season with salt and pepper.

Instant Pot Chicken Soup

Prep time: 10 minutes | Cook time: 30 minutes | Serves 12

1 large onion diced
2 large carrots or 3 small, chopped
1.5 cup green beans chopped into 1 inch pieces
4 garlic cloves minced
1 inch ginger minced
4 pounds whole chicken preferably pasture raised
2 teaspoon sea salt plus more to taste
Cracked black pepper to taste
5 cups water
Chopped green onions, for garnish

1. Place onion, carrots, green beans, garlic, and ginger in the instant pot.
2. Lay the chicken over the vegetables.
3. Sprinkle with salt and pepper.
4. Pour water over everything.
5. Close the lid of the Instant Pot, then set it to "Soup" on high pressure of 30 minutes.
6. Once the soup is finished, the Instant Pot will beep a few times. Wait about 30 minutes for the pressure to go down naturally until you can open the lid.
7. Take out the chicken and debone. You can save the bones to make bone broth.
8. Shred the meat and place back in the instant pot. Stir.
9. Taste and add more salt and pepper, if needed.
10. Serve with chopped green onions sprinkled on top.

Beef Chuck Roast and Beet Borscht

Prep time: 10 minutes | Cook time: 20 minutes | Serves 4

1 large bunch red beets with greens
1¼ pounds (567 g) beef chuck roast, trimmed and cut into ½-inch chunks
1 tablespoon extra-virgin olive oil
Salt and freshly ground black pepper, to taste
2½ cups beef broth
1 yellow onion, chopped
1 teaspoon caraway seeds
1 teaspoon dried dill
1 tablespoon balsamic or red wine vinegar
Optional garnish

1. Wash the beets and the greens well. Peel the beets and cut them into ½-inch pieces; set aside. Finely chop the stems and greens (keep them separate) until you have 1 cup of each; set aside.
2. Toss half the beef with the oil and season generously with salt and pepper. Select SAUTÉ and adjust to MORE/HIGH heat. When the pot is hot, add the seasoned beef and cook, stirring occasionally, until well browned, 4 minutes. Press CANCEL.
3. Add the remaining (unbrowned) beef, the broth, beets, beet stems, onions, caraway, and dill to the pot. (You'll add the beet greens at the end of cooking.) Lock on the lid, select the PRESSURE COOK function, and adjust to HIGH pressure for 15 minutes. Make sure the steam valve is in the "Sealing" position. (Or you can SLOW COOK it—see instructions below.)
4. When the cooking time is up, let the pressure release naturally for 10 minutes and then carefully release the remaining pressure. Add the vinegar and beet greens to the pot. Select SAUTÉ and adjust to MORE/HIGH heat. Cook until the soup is simmering and the greens are tender, 1 minute. Press CANCEL. Season with salt and pepper.

Creamy Asparagus Soup

Prep time: 10 minutes | Cook time: 22 minutes | Serves 12

4 pounds asparagus tough ends trimmed
4 tablespoon ghee or coconut oil for vegan
4 garlic cloves minced
2 yellow onion chopped
2 teaspoon sea salt or more to taste
0.5 teaspoon ground black pepper
10 cups bone broth or chicken broth
2 cup full-fat coconut milk
juice of ½ lemon or more taste

1. Wash the asparagus and chop in half.
2. In a large saucepan, heat ghee over medium heat.
3. Add garlic and onion and sauté until soft, about 2 minutes.
4. Add asparagus, salt, and pepper, and cook stirring for 5 minutes.
5. Pour in bone broth, cover, and let it come to a simmer.
6. Turn down the heat to medium low and simmer for 15 minutes until the asparagus is cooked through and soft.
7. Use an immersion blender to blender the contents until smooth. If you don't have an immersion blender, you can transfer the contents to a regular blender to blend. Return back to the pot.
8. Stir in coconut milk and lemon juice.
9. Taste to add more salt, pepper, and/or lemon juice, before serving.

Beef Borscht Soup

Prep time: 10 minutes | Cook time: 20 minutes | Serves 6

2 pounds (907 g) ground beef
3 beets, peeled and diced
3 stalks of celery, diced
2 large carrots, diced
2 cloves of garlic, diced
1 onion, diced
3 cups shredded cabbage
6 cups beef stock
1 bay leaf
½ tablespoon thyme
Salt and pepper

1. Press the Sauté button on the Instant Pot.
2. Sauté the beef for 5 minutes until slightly golden.
3. Add all the rest of the ingredients in the Instant Pot.
4. Close the lid and press the Manual button.
5. Adjust the cooking time to 15 minutes.
6. Do natural pressure release.

Lime-Orange Brussels Sprouts

Prep time: 10 minutes | Cook time: 8 minutes | Serves 6

1 and ½ pounds (680 g) Brussels
    sprouts, halved
A pinch of salt and black pepper
¼ cup orange juice
1 teaspoon orange zest, grated
1 teaspoon lime zest, grated
1 tablespoon olive oil

1. In your instant pot, combine all the ingredients, toss, put the lid on and cook on High for 8 minutes.
2. Release the pressure naturally for 10 minutes, divide the mix between plates and serve.

Bone Broth in an Instant

Prep time: 10 minutes | Cook time: 20 minutes | Serves 5

2½ pounds beef bones, including short ribs,
    knuckles, oxtails, and more
1 teaspoon extra-virgin olive oil
1 yellow or white onion, quartered
2 celery stalks, quartered
1 carrot, quartered
4 garlic cloves, smashed
1 bay leaf
1 tablespoon apple cider vinegar
2 teaspoons sea salt

1. Preheat the oven to 400°F.
2. Toss the bones with the oil on a baking sheet and roast for 30 minutes.
3. Once cool enough to handle, combine the bones, onion, celery, carrot, garlic, bay leaf, vinegar, salt, and 8 cups of water in the bowl of the Instant Pot.
4. Secure the lid and seal the vent. Select Pressure Cook or Manual and cook on high pressure for 1½ hours, then allow the pressure to naturally release. Open the vent at the top and remove the lid. Press Cancel.
5. Carefully strain the broth using a fine-mesh strainer or cheesecloth. Store in the refrigerator for up to 1 week or in the freezer for up to 3 months.

Sweet Potato and "Pea-not" Stew

Prep time: 5 minutes | Cook time: 20 minutes | Serves 4

2 tablespoons coconut oil or extra-
    virgin olive oil
1 large yellow or white onion, diced
2 large sweet potatoes, peeled and
    cut into 1-inch chunks
⅓ cup sunflower seed butter
1 teaspoon smoked paprika
¼ teaspoon red pepper flakes or ⅛
    teaspoon cayenne pepper
2 cups vegetable broth or water
½ teaspoon sea salt
¼ teaspoon freshly ground black pepper
1 to 2 cups coarsely chopped fresh spinach or kale

1. Select Sauté on the Instant Pot. Heat the oil until it shimmers.
2. Sauté the onion until softened, 2 to 3 minutes, stirring occasionally.
3. Add the sweet potatoes, sunflower seed butter, paprika, red pepper flakes, broth, salt, and black pepper. Stir to combine. Press Cancel.
4. Secure the lid and seal the vent. Select Pressure Cook or Manual and cook on high pressure for 6 minutes, then naturally release the pressure in the pot for 5 minutes. Quick release the remaining pressure in the pot and remove the lid.
5. Stir in the spinach to wilt. Serve and enjoy!

Pumpkin Soup with Fennel and Leeks

Prep time: 5 minutes | Cook time: 20 minutes | Serves 3

2 tablespoons extra-virgin olive oil

1 leek, white and light green parts only, thinly sliced

1 fennel bulb, fronds removed and thinly sliced

4 garlic cloves, coarsely chopped

2 teaspoons smoked paprika

½ teaspoon ground cumin

¼ teaspoon ground nutmeg

1 (15-ounce) can pumpkin puree

4 cups vegetable broth

1 teaspoon sea salt, plus more as needed

¼ teaspoon freshly ground black pepper, plus more as needed

1. Select Sauté on the Instant Pot. Heat the oil until it shimmers.
2. Add the leek, fennel, and garlic. Sauté for 2 to 3 minutes, until the vegetables start to soften. Press Cancel.
3. Add the paprika, cumin, nutmeg, pumpkin puree, broth, salt, and pepper, and stir to combine.
4. Secure the lid and seal the vent. Select Pressure Cook or Manual and cook on high pressure for 5 minutes, then allow the pressure to naturally release for 5 minutes. Quick release the remaining pressure in the pot and remove the lid. Press Cancel.
5. Taste and season with additional salt and pepper as needed. Serve and enjoy!

Appendix 1: Measurement Conversion Chart

MEASUREMENT CONVERSION CHART

VOLUME EQUIVALENTS(DRY)

US STANDARD	METRIC (APPROXIMATE)
1/8 teaspoon	0.5 mL
1/4 teaspoon	1 mL
1/2 teaspoon	2 mL
3/4 teaspoon	4 mL
1 teaspoon	5 mL
1 tablespoon	15 mL
1/4 cup	59 mL
1/2 cup	118 mL
3/4 cup	177 mL
1 cup	235 mL
2 cups	475 mL
3 cups	700 mL
4 cups	1 L

VOLUME EQUIVALENTS(LIQUID)

US STANDARD	US STANDARD (OUNCES)	METRIC (APPROXIMATE)
2 tablespoons	1 fl.oz.	30 mL
1/4 cup	2 fl.oz.	60 mL
1/2 cup	4 fl.oz.	120 mL
1 cup	8 fl.oz.	240 mL
1 1/2 cup	12 fl.oz.	355 mL
2 cups or 1 pint	16 fl.oz.	475 mL
4 cups or 1 quart	32 fl.oz.	1 L
1 gallon	128 fl.oz.	4 L

TEMPERATURES EQUIVALENTS

FAHRENHEIT(F)	CELSIUS(C) (APPROXIMATE)
225 °F	107 °C
250 °F	120 °C
275 °F	135 °C
300 °F	150 °C
325 °F	160 °C
350 °F	180 °C
375 °F	190 °C
400 °F	205 °C
425 °F	220 °C
450 °F	235 °C
475 °F	245 °C
500 °F	260 °C

WEIGHT EQUIVALENTS

US STANDARD	METRIC (APPROXIMATE)
1 ounce	28 g
2 ounces	57 g
5 ounces	142 g
10 ounces	284 g
15 ounces	425 g
16 ounces (1 pound)	455 g
1.5 pounds	680 g
2 pounds	907 g

Appendix 2: Instant Pot Cooking Timetable

Instant Pot Cooking Timetable

Dried Beans, Legumes and Lentils

Dried Beans and Legume	Dry (Minutes)	Soaked (Minutes)
Soy beans	25 – 30	20 – 25
Scarlet runner	20 – 25	10 – 15
Pinto beans	25 – 30	20 – 25
Peas	15 – 20	10 – 15
Navy beans	25 – 30	20 – 25
Lima beans	20 – 25	10 – 15
Lentils, split, yellow (moong dal)	15 – 18	N/A
Lentils, split, red	15 – 18	N/A
Lentils, mini, green (brown)	15 – 20	N/A
Lentils, French green	15 – 20	N/A
Kidney white beans	35 – 40	20 – 25
Kidney red beans	25 – 30	20 – 25
Great Northern beans	25 – 30	20 – 25
Pigeon peas	20 – 25	15 – 20
Chickpeas (garbanzo bean chickpeas)	35 – 40	20 – 25
Cannellini beans	35 – 40	20 – 25
Black-eyed peas	20 – 25	10 – 15
Black beans	20 – 25	10 – 15

Fish and Seafood

Fish and Seafood	Fresh (minutes)	Frozen (minutes)
Shrimp or Prawn	1 to 2	2 to 3
Seafood soup or stock	6 to 7	7 to 9
Mussels	2 to 3	4 to 6
Lobster	3 to 4	4 to 6
Fish, whole (snapper, trout, etc.)	5 to 6	7 to 10
Fish steak	3 to 4	4 to 6
Fish fillet,	2 to 3	3 to 4
Crab	3 to 4	5 to 6

Fruits

Fruits	Fresh (in Minutes)	Dried (in Minutes)
Raisins	N/A	4 to 5
Prunes	2 to 3	4 to 5
Pears, whole	3 to 4	4 to 6
Pears, slices or halves	2 to 3	4 to 5
Peaches	2 to 3	4 to 5
Apricots, whole or halves	2 to 3	3 to 4
Apples, whole	3 to 4	4 to 6
Apples, in slices or pieces	2 to 3	3 to 4

Meat

Meat and Cuts	Cooking Time (minutes)	Meat and Cuts	Cooking Time (minutes)
Veal, roast	35 to 45	Duck, with bones, cut up	10 to 12
Veal, chops	5 to 8	Cornish Hen, whole	10 to 15
Turkey, drumsticks (leg)	15 to 20	Chicken, whole	20 to 25
Turkey, breast, whole, with bones	25 to 30	Chicken, legs, drumsticks, or thighs	10 to 15
Turkey, breast, boneless	15 to 20	Chicken, with bones, cut up	10 to 15
Quail, whole	8 to 10	Chicken, breasts	8 to 10
Pork, ribs	20 to 25	Beef, stew	15 to 20
Pork, loin roast	55 to 60	Beef, shanks	25 to 30
Pork, butt roast	45 to 50	Beef, ribs	25 to 30
Pheasant	20 to 25	Beef, steak, pot roast, round, rump, brisket or blade, small chunks, chuck,	25 to 30
Lamb, stew meat	10 to 15		
Lamb, leg	35 to 45	Beef, pot roast, steak, rump, round, chuck, blade or brisket, large	35 to 40
Lamb, cubes,	10 t0 15		
Ham slice	9 to 12	Beef, ox-tail	40 to 50
Ham picnic shoulder	25 to 30	Beef, meatball	10 to 15
Duck, whole	25 to 30	Beef, dressed	20 to 25

Made in the USA
Las Vegas, NV
26 December 2021